THE
RAT
PEOPLE

The
RAT
PEOPLE

A Journey through
Beijing's Forbidden
Underground

PATRICK SAINT-PAUL
Translated by DAVID HOMEL

ARSENAL PULP PRESS
VANCOUVER

ARSENAL PULP PRESS
Suite 202 – 211 East Georgia St.
Vancouver, BC V6A 1Z6
Canada
arsenalpulp.com

Liberté • Égalité • Fraternité
RÉPUBLIQUE FRANÇAISE

The translation of this book has been completed in partnership with the Cultural Service of the French Embassy in Canada / *en partenariat avec le service culturel de l'Ambassade de France au Canada.*

Canada

The publisher gratefully acknowledges the support of the Government of Canada, and the Government of British Columbia (through the Book Publishing Tax Credit Program), for its publishing activities.

Arsenal Pulp Press acknowledges the xʷməθkʷəy̓əm (Musqueam), Sḵwx̱wú7mesh (Squamish), and səlilwətaʔɬ (Tsleil-Waututh) Nations, custodians of the traditional, ancestral, and unceded territories where our office is located. We pay respect to their histories, traditions, and continuous living cultures and commit to accountability, respectful relations, and friendship.

Front cover design by Oliver McPartlin
Back cover and text design by Jazmin Welch
Copy edited by Shirarose Wilensky
Proofread by Alison Strobel

Printed and bound in Canada

Library and Archives Canada Cataloguing in Publication:
Title: The rat people : a journey through Beijing's forbidden underground / Patrick Saint-Paul ; translated by David Homel.
Other titles: Peuple des rats. English
Names: Saint-Paul, Patrick, author. | Homel, David, translator.
Description: Translation of: Le peuple des rats : dans les sous-sols interdits de la Chine. | Includes bibliographical references.
Identifiers: Canadiana (print) 20200151622 | Canadiana (ebook) 20200151703 |
ISBN 9781551528038 (softcover) | ISBN 9781551528045 (HTML)
Subjects: LCSH: Working poor—China—Beijing—Biography. | LCSH: Working class—China—Beijing—Social conditions. | LCSH: Working class—Housing—China—Beijing. | LCSH: Underground areas—China—Beijing. | LCSH: Rural-urban migration—China—Beijing. | LCSH: Migrant labor—China—Beijing—Biography.
Classification: LCC HD8740.B45 S2513 2020 | DDC 305.5/690951156—dc23

"But the minute there were people around, out came all the words I'd stored up inside, like rats fleeing a nest."

—MO YAN, *Shifu, You'll Do Anything for a Laugh*

CONTENTS

INTRODUCTION

Today's China has definitely buried the "low-profile" and "peaceful rise" philosophy adopted by the prudent Deng Xiaoping in the early 1990s. Xi Jinping, who will presumably rule over the People's Republic until the end of his days, has replaced his predecessor's approach with a dogma of self-assertive power and the restoration of the nation's greatness after the humiliations inflicted by the West in the nineteenth century. Xi's dreams of grandeur have swept away Deng's famous motto *"Tao Guang Yang Hui"*—keep a low profile and bide your time. The West was slow to recognize the Chinese steamroller and understand the consequences of Beijing's strategic aggressiveness.

The most powerful ruler since Mao Zedong, Xi Jinping wants China to be the world's most powerful nation by 2050. Beijing has increased its military budget, now second to that of the United States, by ten percent every year, a clear message as to its strategic intentions. Pushed forward by Xi, China's will to establish regional control will bring its share of conflicts. His imperialist appetites include Hong Kong and Taiwan, and his objective is to become absolute master of the South China Sea, which has created deep concerns for his neighbors. For Xi, the new silk roads are tools of domination that will help advance his counter-model to Western democracy. Through his massive investments in Bangladesh, Pakistan, and central Asia, as well as the Eastern European countries, Greece, and Italy, he intends for China to not only take control of strategic assets but also throw its political weight around.

The European countries did not open their eyes to the dangers of rising Chinese power until long after the Americans did. Absorbed by their domestic crises, concerned with the chaos in the Middle East, they paid no mind to China's quiet advancement. They were blinded by the spectacular mirage of China's GNP and preferred to see it as an El Dorado for their industrial conglomerates. As an empire of smoke and mirrors, China played to their need for illusion. In reality, the Middle Kingdom gives only crumbs to foreign investors in exchange for their technologies, an absolute condition if they want to set up shop there. Over the years, China has become a strategic competitor and a systemic rival.

In Brussels, capital of the European Union, leaders are now fearful that China will attempt to divide and destabilize the EU, by creating a Trojan horse with their billions of dollars of investment, and then impose its own interests. Over the last five years, China's investments in sensitive sectors of Europe's economy have skyrocketed; for example, new technologies like Chinese company Huawei's 5G network bring risks of espionage. The concern becomes even greater while the West looks on, unable to react, as China imposes its counter-model free from democracy. For too long, Western countries believed that the move toward democracy would necessarily follow in the footsteps of economic development. That has not been the case.

The repression of the Tiananmen Square protests destroyed all hopes that China's Communist regime might open up. The "Fifth Modernization," which would have been democracy, is not about to happen. The "dangerous" democratic spirit of spring 1989 created an obsession with control in a regime that believes opening up is tantamount to doubt. Xi will not be the Chinese Gorbachev. He learned his lessons from the collapse of the Soviet Union, and does not want to share the fate of its rulers. He believes the slightest crack, the smallest doubt, could be devastating in a country of nearly 1.4 billion people. To increase the regime's life span, the People's Republic forged its own path: a mix of economic liberalism and political authoritarianism. The concentration of power, the elimination of political rivals under the guise of fighting corruption, the stifling of dissident voices, and the use of cutting-edge technologies for social control are the tools of this new absolutism. And it's all cemented together by the rebirth of ideology, a combination of crypto-Maoism and Confucian tradition.

To confront the Chinese steamroller, US president Donald Trump's counteroffensive resulted in the Thucydides Trap, which occurs when a rising power threatens the established power, making war inevitable, as was the case with Athens and Sparta. The resulting trade war has brought about a dangerous dynamic. Xi Jinping wants to make China so rich and powerful that other countries will have no choice but to bend to its will and show it due respect. Trump, who promised to make America great again, is on a collision course with Xi by rejecting the rule of technology transfer China imposes on companies that want to penetrate its market and by imposing tariffs on Chinese exports. The Trump administration has identified China's Achilles heel—the Middle Kingdom believed it could isolate itself in certain sectors, while benefiting from globalization in others and receiving all the advantages of its status as a developing economy.

The economic miracle that led to China's rebirth would not have been possible without the Rat People: generations of *mingong*, migrant workers, who have been sacrificed. Peasants move from the country to live underground beneath the great cities and provide cheap labor for the spectacular development of the new empire. To make sure growth stays vigorous, by 2025, Beijing intends to push 250 million peasants into the cities, creating the greatest human migration in history. This exodus from rural to urban is causes considerable human suffering. Despite housing and education offered by the central government, this next generation of sacrificial victims will have all the trouble in the world adapting to city life. Beijing's challenge will be to help their children enter a more modern China.

—**PATRICK SAINT-PAUL**, August 2019

CHAPTER 1

WANDERING RATS IN THE KINGDOM OF CONSUMER DECADENCE

The lutz is executed with precision and elegance. Wrapped in her short fur vest, the young figure skater with braided hair weaves backward down the ice, her hands firmly on her hips, to the sound of Barbra Streisand singing "Memory." From her spot by the glass balustrade, her mother is watching the young prodigy with one eye, the other on her latest model, gold-colored iPhone. Other parents have used the hour-long lesson to go shopping and are now waiting patiently with large Louis Vuitton, Hermès, and Prada bags at their feet.

Sheltered from the pollution that hangs heavy over Beijing more than half the year, the privileged kids of the new economic superpower can go skating all year round in the biggest luxury mall in the Chinese capital. Measuring 800 square meters (8,600 square feet), the place has earned the name Le Cool. The showroom of the Chinese economic explosion of the last thirty years, the three towers of the China World Trade Center, begun in 1985 and finished in 2010, dominate the ultramodern glass-and-steel skyscrapers of the Central Business District, which the city's inhabitants have abbreviated to CBD. In an effort to welcome foreigners, China World humbly defines itself as "the place where China meets the world." In the China World Mall, Red princes, the super-wealthy heirs of the Communist regime, tucked into their perfectly tailored Italian suits, stroll through the 100,000 square meters (some 1.1 million square feet) of marble hallways, stretching over four floors, stopping to glance in blasé fashion at the windows of the 300 luxury boutiques: Berluti, Dior, Moncler, Leica ... The wives and girlfriends of these overnight fortunes built on *guanxi*—the indispensable network of connections, with the Chinese Communist Party at the center, necessary to anyone's success in the People's Republic—can satisfy their consumer cravings here, too.

A very discreet army of hardworking employees looks after the site's upkeep. These women are known as *ayi*, or "aunt," blue-uniformed cleaners who see to the floors and windows, while others, in gray uniforms, both men and women, hand out soap and paper towels in the restrooms. These are the underlings of Chinese prosperity. Their lives are no fairy tale. Almost all of them are *mingong*, who by the tens of millions have deserted the poor rural districts and poured into the big cities in search of jobs, forming the greatest human migration in history. The wealth of the entire nation that is poised to become the number one world economy is built on the shoulders of these laboring masses.

In Beijing, like in most large Chinese centers, the property prices have exploded, and countless workers employed in the service sector, on construction sites, or with menial tasks paid in starvation wages wait for a better opportunity. The forgotten faces of growth, they are often exploited and considered second-class citizens. Their fate can be compared to the working class in European cities during the industrial revolution of the nineteenth century. Seven million *mingong*, out of 21 million inhabitants, contribute to the exuberant growth of the capital city, where they have come in hope of a better life, transforming the country into the global economic powerhouse it is now. Meanwhile, they live underground—literally. This population from the four corners of the country has adopted the nickname they've been given: the *shuzu*, or "rat tribe." In Beijing, the tribe lives in countless basement rooms, and even in sewers. More than 1 million of them, according to estimates, subsist in Beijing's belly. With no *hukou*, or residence permit, the paper needed to access all forms of the social safety net, including health insurance and schools for their children, they don't have even the most basic rights. Stuck at the bottom of the ladder, their only hope is to move up a rung or two.

"Migrant workers live underground, like rats, in the same conditions as rodents, with very little or no natural light, in a damp habitat," explains Lu Huitin, professor of sociology at Peking University. "Which is how these people earned their nickname. But unlike rats, it is very bad for human health to live in those conditions. They develop skin diseases and suffer psychological problems. Depression is common among the rat tribe. And accidents happen frequently: fire, floods, asphyxiation, which cause many deaths every year in these underground dwellings. And migrant workers, either young people with a college degree looking for a job or youth laboring for poor wages, the ones who inhabit the bowels of the capital, are far from dangerous. They play an essential role in Beijing's economic activity. Yet when you work in the center of the city, it is almost impossible to find decent lodgings. The *mingong* hope to improve their standard of living and, one day, dwell on the surface. But they see that their salaries are not getting any better, and that they will stay deep in their holes."

At China World, more than anywhere else, day and night, the rat people rub shoulders with the Chinese dream of old glories restored, of power and prosperity. But those things will never be theirs. They are on the front lines of China's ideological bankruptcy, which keeps them down in a country with outrageous inequalities, even as it proclaims the virtues of Communist egalitarianism.

Any attempt to strike up a conversation with an *ayi* at China World is met with an averted or frightened gaze. These women are curious about the outside world, but they are allowed to communicate with it only to render their services.

"I can't talk to you," a young woman says, her mop and pail in one hand, increasing her pace. "I don't have the right. Cameras are everywhere. They are always watching us. The management is very strict here. We can never stop working."

She possesses nothing, but she is afraid of losing everything. The pay is significantly better at China World than elsewhere, and working here is considered a privilege in the universe of human rats. No one will speak to us. Our little maneuver has been sniffed out. We are not here to buy, like everyone else. We walk slowly, nonchalant, in search of human prey. But as soon as we approach, the human rats take fright and flee.

Discouraged, I'm ready to admit defeat after several days of fruitless hunting. I feel like a fisherman returning home empty-handed, but I decide to cast the line one more time. I spot a young woman, a maintenance worker, wearing a look somewhat less closed than her sisters. She slows as she walks by, looking down so that her eyes will not meet mine. But she agrees to talk to me. She says her name is Shen, and she left Sichuan province to seek her fortune in Beijing eight years ago. She was eighteen at the time and had just finished school. She has been working at China World for five years. Her red hands clutching her mop, she smiles sweetly, then looks around anxiously. Shen has lived east of the city for the last two years, near the Communication University of China, a half-hour subway ride from work. She is renting an eight-square-meter (eighty-six-square-foot) room with another woman, underground, for 800 yuan (US$115) a month. According to her, she is lucky to have a vent, which means she can breathe air from outside during the scorching summer days. The two roommates have a hot plate to cook their meals in their subterranean chamber and access to a shared bathroom, where the minutes they spend in the shower are counted out on a prepaid card.

These kinds of lodgings, which rent at half the cost of an equivalent space above ground, were created back in the era of Mao Zedong. When tensions between China and the Soviet Union were at their height, in the Cold War days, when Beijing was fighting it out with Moscow for ideological supremacy over the Eastern Bloc, Mao ordered the construction of a vast network of underground shelters in Beijing. In 1969, as armed border skirmishes between the two countries became more frequent along the natural line of demarcation of the Amur River, Mao launched a program to dig deep tunnels to protect the People's Republic in case of Russian air raids. In Beijing, 300,000 people took part in this campaign, building 20,000 shelters. This scheme built a complete underground city made up of passages linking bomb shelters to important points in the city above, or schools, hospitals, factories, stores, restaurants, theaters, and a skating rink.

After Mao died, the strategy of opening the country up to international trade set in motion by Deng Xiaoping led to more pragmatic economic policies, and the underground spaces were turned into money-makers. The government's civil defense department ordered the shelters to be commercialized, so some

800 lodgings were created in the entrails of the city, along with hospitals, supermarkets, and movie houses. In 1996, the government adopted a law decreeing that every new building in the megacity had to include underground space for people. A veritable city on several lower levels began to sprout in these spaces. Real estate fever, the source of recurring popular resentment, and not only among the poorest sections of the population, pushed the Beijing *mingong* into these lodgings, which were often harmful to their health. The average monthly salary for a *mingong* is about 3,000 yuan (US$425). But in Beijing, the most expensive city in continental China, real estate fever has driven up the purchase price for a property to 31,465 yuan (nearly US$4,500) per square meter (around ten square feet), an amount no *mingong* could afford. To make things worse, according to official Chinese media, the average price for housing in the capital corresponds to 13.3 times the average annual income. Note that the World Bank states that the gap between income and the price of lodging should not exceed a ratio of one to five. Over the years, the authorities have ordered the closure of the most outdated and dangerous underground residences. However, the city estimates that 6,000 subterranean lodgings are still rented to this day. To exploit such spaces commercially has been outlawed for several years. But, as is often the case in China, where rules and laws are secondary to pragmatism, to encourage economic growth or allow a business that belongs to some corrupt bureaucrat to prosper, a gray zone has developed. Some of the underground spaces have been entrusted to "managers," whereas others have been ordered to shut down ... while the local government continues to tolerate their existence.

Shen left her village instead of spending the rest of her life working in the fields for starvation wages. She could have gone to one of the midsize cities closer to home, but the pay would hardly have been better. So she resolved to take the great leap and move to the capital. Between the beginning of the economic opening up in 1979 and 2002, some 400 million rural citizens emerged from poverty, but that didn't lessen the increasing inequalities between country and city people. Peasants were facing greater difficulties in their daily lives, and they responded by migrating en masse to urban centers. Some 270 million peasants moved to the cities over three decades. It is estimated that some 8 million peasants leave the countryside every year in search of work. More than half the population of China lives in urban centers. And according to demographers' projections, by 2030, 1 billion Chinese will be city dwellers—300 million more than today.

Next to President Xi Jinping's dream of recovering Chinese grandeur, Shen's ambitions are considerably more modest: to live a little better than her parents, peasants haunted by the fear of a poor harvest that happened when they were younger. Haunted also by the fear of their land being confiscated by some small-time corrupt bureaucrat, and being sent to one of those barracks villages reserved for farmers whose land was expropriated. Shen decided not to wait for that to happen.

"Life isn't as hard for me as for my parents. I never go hungry. I have heat and I can watch TV," she tells me with a timid smile, wringing hands reddened and chapped by the cleaning products she uses.

But confined to the fishbowl of Beijing's underground chambers, Shen's life lies light-years away from the new China symbolized by her workplace.

◆

In Sanlitun, Beijing's most upscale neighborhood, a stone's throw from the CBD, a white Bentley can hardly hold its own against the candy-colored Ferrari and the glitter-green Lamborghini parked in front of the 3.3, another luxury shopping center. Weighed down by her Louis Vuitton bag, in a miniskirt, mile-high heels, and crystal-inlay blue nails, its driver is quite the sight. Rich Beijing women love their cars. To stand out in the city, whose unbridled growth has offered its well-born children colossal wealth, money must speak its name ostentatiously. Each prestige automobile tells a story of individual success, a sort of mini-Olympics on the Beijing stage, where China engages in an orgy of spending that no other country has ever seen.

There's no chance that Xiaoyun will be dazzled by the new China, yet nothing escapes the attention of the blind street musician who's been working the Sanlitun district, since arriving from Henan province fifteen years ago. He plays the *erhu*, his traditional but rather banged-up instrument that has a medieval tone, incongruous against the soundtrack of a developing capital city drunk on its own prosperity: the engines growling, the car doors slamming, the high heels punishing the sidewalk. The musician depends on the generosity of passersby, and he rails good-heartedly against this new individualistic society.

"I owe my life to the generous hearts of Beijing people," he says. "I'm lucky because they have become more civilized. At the beginning, I couldn't even cross the street against the river of bicycles. When the cars started showing up, people drove like they were crazy. To survive fifteen years in Beijing is a miracle if you're blind." The advent of luxury cars did not escape his attention, however. "The noise that the motors and the doors make is different," he points out. "People drive a lot slower to show off, so crossing the street isn't as dangerous."

The city has gotten richer, but Xiaoyun has not bettered his lot. On the contrary. The cost of rent has exploded, and he's had to move from a run-down two-room apartment above ground to an underground space.

"A lot of people in Beijing are rich now, but that has made them colder and more individualistic. Obsessed with money and success," he says regretfully. "The more money they have, the less generous they are."

Xiaoyun's father was a math teacher in his village school. He brought Xiaoyun to Beijing and Tiananmen Square when the boy was a teenager, and he has worshipped his father ever since. Totally lost after he died, Xiaoyun returned to the city to drown his sorrows in alcohol. And he never left.

Like the other human rats, he inhabits a swampy underground room whose walls stink of the sweat of the other inhabitants. But he does not belong to the tribe. Too unproductive, too raggedy, he is one of the few to survive in this environment hostile to idleness. Like most people of his generation born blind in rural districts, he learned early on to play the *erhu*, a sort of two-stringed violin, but his life in the Beijing streets made it impossible for him to truly master his instrument, and he has never played in a traditional Chines opera.

But in today's China, where everyone thinks they have a shot at the dream, Xiaoyun goes on believing in his lucky star. He recently put together a group of three musicians from his village in Henan.

"In Beijing, life is no good for me. I'm going to join up with my group and play weddings and funerals. There's money to be made. One day I will be rich."

"How can you be so sure?"

"People who are getting married want to spread their money around, even if they don't have any. And dead people have to do whatever they can to draw a crowd to their funeral so they'll be remembered as somebody respectable. Some even rent strippers to dance on their grave and attract people. Hiring a traditional music group is the bare minimum."

In China, as in many Asian societies, social status is borne out at the funeral, measured by the number of mourners. But the government has put an end to excesses at the wake. Shows featuring nude women that once often accompanied burials, especially in the countryside in southern China, are now prohibited. A hopeful sign for Xiaoyun, at least in theory.

◆

In China World, the luxury boutique showrooms are like a glass ceiling for Shen. They display a world that is inaccessible. The gowns and the handbags that cost two years of her salary do not attract her. But, somewhat ashamed, she admits to admiring the goods on the shelves of the supermarket on the ground floor.

"I've never bought anything here, it's all too expensive. People like us don't shop here. It's not made for us," she declares.

Her words cause a certain discomfort. My family considered this luxury grocery store a lifesaver when we first came to Beijing. My wife discovered her favorites from France: La Mère Poulard cookies, Côte d'Or chocolate, and jars of Nutella—our number one weapon against our children's homesickness. Ripped away from the creature comforts of their European life, they were thrown into my mad Chinese adventure with all its passion but with its very rough edges, too. We spent a fortune on these products, luxury items in China. I enjoyed the guilty pleasure of savoring a chunk of Roquefort cheese when I returned from my forays into deepest China, where I subsisted on fried noodles, dumplings, and soup.

The incongruity of the situation set off some self-questioning. Was it not indecent to interview people living under the earth, to try to understand their existence without sharing it, their daily lives, at least for a time? How could I convince them to trust me?

As if to free me from these thoughts, Shen added, "Actually, I did come here once. Five years ago, when I arrived here, the supermarket gave me a coupon for a free item. I didn't know what to choose."

In the end, she reached for a chocolate bar. She had never tasted the stuff.

Chinese people who have made their fortune, and do not want to risk getting poisoned by local food, since many have died eating it, find a safe place in this luxury food emporium. Strawberries from Galilee, cherries from Chile, and mangos and pineapples from the Philippines offer healthy alternatives to toxic domestic fruit. Cans of powdered baby formula at 500 yuan (US$70) replace Chinese milk laced with melamine that has killed children. To wash down dinner, there's nothing better than a Château Pétrus 2006 at 34,000 yuan (US$4,850), or a Lafite 2011, the preferred tipple of millionaires and top party brass at 25,840 yuan (US$3,685).

During her break, Shen leads us into the labyrinth of hallways reserved for staff, to continue the conversation far from the cameras' prying eyes. She works at several jobs to make a decent living. In the evening, she cleans offices in a tower.

Two security guards wearing dark suits and earpieces burst in just as she is about to give us her telephone number so that we could organize a visit to her mousehole. Her superior sounded the alarm.

"We saw everything you did on the cameras. You have violated the labor laws," they insist.

When Chinese workers mention the rights granted them by law, it means they are at the end of their rope. Knowing they have no chance of winning, they generally avoid such drastic measures. But when a security guard uses labor laws to enforce his boss's authority, it's no laughing matter.

"No employee who works here lives in the basement," declares the head of the work crew: black suit, black tie, red-faced with anger. "Everyone who works here has decent housing."

With the surveillance cameras looking on, the man is exceedingly firm. His superiors will be in a position to judge his convictions. I try to negotiate a few more minutes with Shen, to note down her cell phone number, but my efforts are in vain. Her head has disappeared between her shoulders, and she is all but paralyzed. After two years in China, I have learned that nothing good can come from it when a person is in that position. The rest of the scenario goes according to plan: we are kicked out by the security tough guys.

Shen slips away like a mouse and goes back to work. Her head down, ears scarlet, she averts her eyes from the spectacle of a *laowai*, a foreigner, being pushed toward the exit without resisting. Clutching her mop, she breathes in shallow gasps. We understand that our days of wandering through China World are over, and that we will never see Shen again. We came to this temple of conspicuous consumption because it seemed to be the ideal place to understand that gap between the modern country with its upper class and the ones propping up the prosperity, living at the bottom.

"Don't bother coming back. If you do, the police will lock you up. Do you think we're stupid?" security man #1 adds, playing his role to perfection, with a virile shove toward the door as the cameras look on.

CHAPTER 2

OBSTACLE COURSE

I understand the problem. I went terribly off course when I decided to investigate the rat people. The obstacles are too great and too numerous. During my first journalistic foray into a Beijing basement, I was kicked out after a few minutes without a semblance of good manners. The underground world is a secret place whose residents are unwilling to describe their living conditions and try to cover their tracks so that they don't lose the little they have gained through work and determination—a roof over their heads, no matter how wretched. And the people who manage those places, navigating that Chinese gray zone between illegality and what the authorities tolerate, are in no hurry to surrender the keys to their labyrinths.

What hope do I have to get more access? My blond hair leaves me no options. When I started this undertaking, I thought of the German journalist Günter Wallraff, who went undercover in the 1980s to expose and denounce xenophobia against Turkish migrant workers, and who told of his experiences in a book called *Lowest of the Low*. But I had to face the facts. I would never be able to change my appearance enough to pass for Chinese. And my rudimentary Mandarin would only allow me to remain mute, whereas Wallraff was able to adopt the Turkish German accent.

My first involuntary immersion in a foreign culture, in 1999, was hardly a success. I was kidnapped by a group of kids no more than twelve years old, armed with Kalashnikovs. The incident took place in the Sierra Leone jungles, not far from Freetown, at the height of the civil war, in the middle of Operation No Living Thing, which left more than 6,000 dead and tens of thousands of amputees in the space of a few weeks. The child soldiers, coerced by the rebels and the head of their group, took me for a white mercenary, or a spy. I had all the trouble in the world convincing them I was a journalist.

My first years as a journalist were spent covering armed conflicts, trying to understand the mechanisms of human folly, and how life, or some semblance of normality, could continue in wartime. Thrown into tragic situations, at times close to the source of absolute evil, I learned to keep a healthy distance, almost by instinct. I suppose distance is necessary if you have to witness a young man high on drugs forcing a nine-year-old child to cut off the arms of peasants in Sierra Leone, under threat of death. Or watch children fleeing bullets in Gaza, or see old villagers in the Ivory Coast burned alive. With the same remove, I gazed upon young executioners, sordid torturers, and magnificent heroes. I descended into darkness and described what I saw objectively, without ever creating relationships, in a desire to avoid emotional involvement.

To tell the story of the *shuzu* is a new challenge. I have to move these bottom dogs to accept me, enter their personal space, and convince them to trust me with the keys to their lives. All the while knowing that it's impossible for me to be one of them, and that the Chinese are wary of anything foreign. My challenge is to pass as a sociologist with a passion for China, or a writer, or the head of some company who was looking for some place to put up his underpaid employees ... anything but a journalist, the creature that inspires the greatest distrust among the Chinese. My cover fluctuates, and is fragile.

I can't pass as a China specialist or a researcher working for a local university. I have to turn to Duoyou, my Chinese assistant from work, and friend, to help me with translation. But can I make him see that I'm not interested in certain questions for their sake but rather for the comments and reactions the person I'm interviewing might have? Duoyou is an excellent interview translator, but will he be able to listen to several conversations at once and get everything that might escape me?

How can I approach people low on the social ladder and be accepted by them? I have no idea. Yet they awake in me a new and human curiosity. I want to understand how they can endure such conditions. I want to learn what they feel as the country prospers. I would love to know what they think of the Communist Party, and if seeds of rebellion are growing inside them. Will they shake the country one day by demanding democracy, or by simply standing up for their rights? What are their hopes for their children? What do they know about the West? Do they sense they belong to an economic power? A close encounter with their world seems all but impossible.

Being a journalist in China is a challenge in itself. My days at the office are broken by visits from state security agents. When I discover two somber-faced cops in jeans and black leather jackets, accompanied by a charming lady translator, I know no good can come from such a visit. After the usual comments about the excellent relations between our two countries and the excellent quality of my newspaper, they circled their prey, moving ever closer with each pass.

"We suggest you do not attend your meeting at three p.m.," they tell me the day I am to meet Ding Zilin, the leader of an activist group of mothers who lost children during the bloody repression at Tiananmen Square on June 4, 1989—an absolute taboo subject.

This sort of impromptu appearance ratchets up the paranoia of journalists working in the country. If there was ever any doubt about whether we were under surveillance, that doubt is gone. Every phone conversation, every email, is inspected. The police know the exact time, place, and identity of the people I meet.

A surreal exchange follows, which is an opportunity to find out more. Playing the fool is the best strategy in these situations.

"My three p.m. meeting," I begin. "What meeting?"

"The one about the sensitive date," answers the police officer, who must carry the message through the interpreter. The other police officer is there only to keep an eye on the first.

The authorities never say the date "June 4, 1989," or "the repression of the student movement," though both phrases keep them busy most of the year. When they are forced to refer to the army's massacre of the students, embarrassment hangs heavy.

"The sensitive date?" I ask, looking stunned.

The police officer is losing his patience. "Yes, you know very well. The events of June 4. We know you are working on something."

"It's the twenty-fifth anniversary of Tiananmen Square. I would have trouble explaining to my paper why I wasn't going to talk about it."

"Yes, but we suggest you not attend your meeting with Mrs Ding. She is going to ask you a favor. That will be bad for you."

"There's nothing illegal about going to visit her. I'm not going there to do her a favor. I'll ask her questions and she'll answer and I'll take notes. That's all. Do you want me to tell my employer, who maintains an office in Beijing, that I'm not going to work because someone suggested I don't? Put yourself in my position. If I suggested that you not do your job, would you agree because you wanted me to like you, even if that meant you'd have trouble with your boss? If you decide to prevent me from going to my meeting, that's different. I can't do anything about that. But if you think it's worth creating an incident because of a meeting with a harmless old lady, that's up to you."

On this day, I am lucky enough to encounter someone who has some brains, and who thinks it better not to risk causing a scandal in the middle of the celebration of fifty years of diplomatic relations between the People's Republic and France. With no results to show their boss, the two police officers have to settle for harassing my assistant, threatening her and her family with any number of things. She listens, unimpressed. After seventeen years of brave and faithful service to the Beijing office of the Parisian newspaper *Le Figaro*, she received her open sesame: a Canadian visa. She boarded the plane with no regrets, considering the direction her country has taken since President Xi Jinping came to power.

To have any chance of meeting Mrs Ding, I decide to go see her in January. Every spring, as June 4 draws near, the government sends her on a forced vacation to a hotel on Hainan Island, in the southern reaches of the country, far from foreign journalists. As it does with everyone with a connection to the "sensitive date." She is one of those people, gifted with exceptional courage, who will still speak with journalists and not hide her feelings.

Many ordinary citizens close up tight as a drum as soon as a foreigner wants to talk about a sensitive subject with them, especially the rat people, who might be kicked out of their meager lodgings. Trying to get the inhabitants of these sad and scandalous chambers to open up will be my greatest challenge yet. Unlike victims who believe they have something to gain by bringing a dark truth to light, the rats have everything to lose.

Journalists working in China are constantly playing a cat-and-mouse game with the authorities. To have any chance of completing a story, they need to improvise and work fast, and hope they can outrun them. Like any bureaucratic system, the inertia of those in power can be our ally. But when we get caught cozying up to a taboo subject, we hit an unmovable wall of polite refusal. The police officer or party official will always offer us a cup of tea before gently showing us the door, even as he promises to organize a lavish dinner "very soon," because "we are good friends now." To get to know the rat people, I will have to break one of the fundamental rules of journalism as it is practiced in China: I am going to return to the same places over and over again to meet the same people. Do I even have a snowball's chance in hell?

Suddenly, a miracle! I find myself face-to-face with a man who spent ten years of his life deep in a sewer. I can't let on too much, just enough to convince him to break down the protective shell that made it possible for him to hold out that long. Duoyou made the contact; he's a true magician. Despite his casual manner, our common adventure has changed him into a hunter who has tracked down this "rat man" and persuaded him to meet us.

CHAPTER 3

A SEWER RAT IN THE HUMAN WORLD

Wang Xiuqing knows the Chinese police well; he played cat and mouse with them for a decade. They showed up one dark, freezing morning in the winter of 2008 in front of the sewer grate that had been his home for the last ten years. One of the uniformed men released a German shepherd from its cage and sent it to sniff out the hole, before pushing Wang into the dog's cage and taking him to the police station. The People's Republic was readying itself for the Olympics, which set off a giant charm offensive, to showcase the New China in a costly burst of expenditures meant to propel the country into the same league as the great world powers. No way was a flea-ridden bottom dog like Wang going to spoil the party.

At the venerable of age of fifty-four, with a gravitas that would inspire respect among young people, Wang's dignity took a beating that day, and he doesn't mind admitting it. Frail looking, with small, quick eyes, and wearing a brand-new blue windbreaker, Wang pulls off his baseball cap to scratch his head. He puts it back on, tilting it toward the back, and gives a pained smile.

"Dignity? I didn't have an ounce left when that happened. Everyone's looking for dignity, but dignity isn't for everyone."

Wang tells his story, more than a little downhearted. I imagine he felt worse when the police pushed him into the cage. What human being could tolerate that? I soon discover an exceptional man who is never ashamed of his situation. A man who never gives up.

Some thirty migrants were living in sewers near the one that sheltered Wang, the biggest in the city, close to the Metropark Lido Hotel in the upscale Chaoyang district, in the very center of the capital. The local government abruptly decided to expel those people one cold morning in January 2014, and the passageways were quickly closed down.

Paradoxically, it was Wang Xiuqing's lucky day. His extraordinary story attracted the attention of the government TV network China Central Television (CCTV), and they did a story on him. Then a Beijing university offered him a stable job as a maintenance man. He repairs tables and chairs, looks after the campus gardens, slaps on fresh paint when the walls start peeling. The school pays him 3,000 yuan (US$425) a month, and he is fed and housed ... in a basement room.

Meanwhile, the Beijing police sealed the door of his former dwelling. "It was this one," he says, pointing to a concrete slab the size of a gravestone. "I chose it for the location, next to a taxi station. And because I could stretch out completely. It was paradise in winter."

His rathole was situated at the foot of a concrete building, a giant grayish bunker that, after twenty years, still stood unfinished.

Finding a more comfortable spot as a squatter inside never occurred to Wang.

"The government wouldn't have let me. There were guards inside," he says.

The government closed its eyes for ten years when it came to his spot at the bottom of a hole, but squatting in the carcass of a building would have meant crossing a line, which is a form of injustice he prefers not to comment on. Would someone in another country have revolted against the system? Would there have been a union or an association to defend his rights? In China, such a thing is impossible. The Communist Party prohibits all protests. It is easier to find people interested in saving dogs threatened with euthanasia than to find ones ready to help men crushed by the system. The party brass and their families have made fortunes by making the jump to unchecked capitalism, wherein the social safety net is nonexistent. During the three decades of double-figure growth, they leaned on the battalions of *mingong* for the cheap labor that is indispensable to rapid economic development. Wang's is an extreme case, but the party hasn't thought twice about sentencing millions of people to poverty in its thirst for wealth that, little by little, has overtaken Communist ideals.

"I don't have the knowledge to talk about what the government does," Wang claims, putting on an idiotic look, rolling his eyes until his features are distorted.

"Good work, Mr Wang. Have you ever considered a career in acting?" I say.

Wang bursts out laughing after putting on a show of not understanding. Then he tries a new act: the shifty real estate agent praising the high points of his former habitat located three meters (ten feet) underground. In winter, it is always toasty down there because of the hot-water pipes that run through it ... Don't worry about the toxic fumes and the rusty pipes that could burst at any time. Wang likes to boast that he's healthy as an ox, even while admitting he had trouble breathing down in his pit because of the low oxygen levels and the damp that would creep into his bones ... To fight the poor environment, he put blankets down on the floor, a kind of makeshift mattress, but they quickly absorbed the moisture and would never dry, and soon mold set in. Too small to be habitable, a neighboring hole was equipped with boiling-hot pipes on which he placed water bottles to heat up for the morning. Hangers attached to the walls of his hole served as a closet for the few items of clothing he owned. To get his bed in order, he would light a candle in the evening—briefly, so as not to be spotted. Wang could keep his cell phone charged thanks to the guards at the Japanese school next door, who would plug it in for him. An empty bottle was his toilet.

"As soon as my body slipped into the hole, it adapted perfectly well, and the need to go number two disappeared completely," he tells us with a certain pride.

He had one bulwark against loneliness: his transistor radio that brought him news and plays. Wang had no contact with the women who lived in nearby sewers, though there were nearly a couple dozen of them.

"They came from the provinces in southern China, faraway places. I didn't understand the way they talked. Besides, they were beggars, parasites. They had no pride."

"So you were better than them?"

"There's no comparison," Wang replies. "They would beg, while I worked every day to feed my wife and three children, who stayed behind in the village."

Wang Xiuqing belongs to the Red generation that grew up under Mao Zedong and experienced the upheaval of the People's Republic, from the great famine to economic opening up and unchecked growth, not to mention the Cultural Revolution. He belongs to the first generation of *mingong*, known for their ability to "swallow bitterness," as the Chinese expression goes. For ten years, he swallowed rivers of bitter potion, as if it were his due. Wang would awake at three in the morning, as the night taxis were beginning to line up at the station close by. He would start washing the cars for five to seven yuan (seventy-five cents to a dollar) per vehicle.

"The taxi police would show up around eight. I had to hide because it was illegal work," he says. "But I knew dozens of drivers, and they hired me. Washing their cars kept me busy until noon."

Next, Wang would offer his services to private individuals. Washing their cars was better paid, from 10 to 15 yuan (US$1.50–2.15), but those customers were not as regular. On a good day, Wang could make 80 to 100 yuan (US$11.50–14.25). By the end of the month, he had accumulated 2,000 yuan (US$285). Generally, he got along on one meal a day.

"Itinerant vendors sell off the meals meant for the construction workers in the area when they don't eat them. For five yuan every day I had rice and vegetables. And sometimes a little meat for one or two yuan more."

During the heart of winter, when the temperature hovered between minus-ten and minus-twenty degrees Celsius (fifteen to minus-five degrees Fahrenheit) for weeks at a time, Wang had to force himself to go out.

"My hands were red and swollen, and I got frostbite," he says, showing us the damage. "But if I stayed down in my hole, it would be like dying and giving up on my family. I would fight the cold by jumping up and down in place and drinking warm water. When it really got too cold and I couldn't take it anymore, I took shelter in my little paradise, my hot spot. The drivers would come looking for me and offer me work."

When I consider the trips I took on my electric bike on winter mornings from my apartment to the office, my admiration for Wang knows no bounds. After ten minutes, I reached my well-heated office tower, but despite the heavy parka that protected me from the icy wind, I was frozen solid. To face down that kind of cold is a heroic exploit.

On this spring morning, cool breezes have swept away the pollution that covers the city most of the year, and the sky is blue. Shivering as I stand before his hole, I try to imagine how, in the twenty-first century, a human being could tolerate those kinds of living conditions. What person in Europe would have withstood living in a hole in harsh winter temperatures, for ten years, without completely giving up? Without complaining about their conditions and while keeping their hope and determination intact?

The summers were even more trying. With the stifling heat, humidity, and heavy rains, Wang's little paradise turned into hell. He moved out into the streets, seeking a patch of thick grass during heat waves and bridges that offered protection when downpours beat down on Beijing.

"At first, it was easy," he remembers. "We could sleep in the parks. But with the Olympics there were guards everywhere, and they chased us away. And the cops wouldn't let us sleep in the street. They throw their weight around and don't care about our rights."

Beijing is no Calcutta or New Delhi. Tourists and university professors who visit the Chinese capital always remark on the fact that there are no slums, unlike the big cities in India or the developing Asian countries. In Beijing, poverty is hidden underground. And when it ventures up to the surface, it is beaten down. To help his government save face, Wang spent long nights wandering the streets, then collapsing onto a bit of grass, before being chased off it by a police officer. Exhaustion tormented his body. Time seemed even more endless than during the icy days of winter.

Sometimes, a charitable taxi driver would let him sleep for a few hours on the back seat of his cab.

"There were a few drivers whose cars didn't run all night. They knew me enough to trust me with their keys. I slept a few hours, then washed the car so they would get it back nice and clean in the morning."

Wang considers himself to be patriotic, but the system forced him into gray zones, making him walk the fine line between what is legal and the limited leeway doled out by the police. He always made sure not to find himself on the wrong side.

"Sometimes my belly ached with hunger," he says. "But I never stole. Not one yuan, not even an apple or an egg from a market stall. Because even if I made very little, I was my family's only source of income. If I went to prison, they wouldn't have anything to eat. Besides, it is dishonorable to steal."

Wang's life changed two years ago, but he is quick to insist that he could go back to his old life if he had to. The taxi drivers honk a greeting when they see him.

"Hey, Xiuqing, you got it made now?" a driver asks, holding out a cigarette.

"You bet! I sleep in every morning until seven. Does your boss let you sleep at night?"

"I'm not lucky like you. I work from midnight to noon. Shitty hours."

Even with all his modesty, Wang has become a hero. He is a star in the powerful Chinese social media, but his life was not changed as radically by online activity as it would have been in North America or Europe.

Over ten years, he estimates he was able to save 36,000 yuan (US$5,150) by living in a sewer. In the Beijing underground, entry-level rents begin at 300 yuan (US$40) a month. At that price, inhabitants cannot expect decent lodgings. Yet Wang never enjoyed the fruits of his sacrifice. Too poor to marry the mother of his children, he decided to tie the knot once a friend told him that after five years of marriage, he could benefit from her rights as a Beijing resident if she came to the capital. Wang comes from Hebei province, not far from the city. His *hukou* is linked to his native province, so he cannot access social services or free health insurance in Beijing. But after saying "I do," Wang got signed up, along with his son and two daughters.

Next thing he knew, the local government fined him 70,000 yuan (US$10,000) for having twice violated the one-child policy. It never occurred to him to protest. Surviving the Beijing hierarchy at the very bottom of the ladder is a complex undertaking that demands extraordinary adaptive powers mixed with inexhaustible fatalism. Rebelling would mean a possible prison sentence, not to mention that friends and neighbors would turn against Wang out of fear of the authorities. With Wang locked up, it would be a death sentence, by starvation, for his family.

"The system is the way it is," Wang states tonelessly. "It's nether bad nor good. Neither fair nor unfair. Every *mingong* knows the rules of the game before they come to Beijing. We're here because there is no more work in our villages, and in the city, we can make enough money to provide a comfortable life back home. Everyone wins: the bosses who pay us low wages, and us, even if we live in bad conditions."

His children are his absolute priority and his reason to live, as well as the reason for his sacrifices.

"When I'm a nobody, stuck at the bottom of my hole, I think of them. They are my dignity. My only goal is to make it possible for them to get an education that will help them have a better life."

◆

The idea that we might go to his family's house in his village of Yaoling, ninety kilometers (fifty-five miles) north of Beijing in Huairou district, does not appeal to Wang Xiuqing.

"My house is a ruin. You couldn't even sit down to eat. I don't have enough chairs," he said, trying to warn me off.

The financial argument finally convinces him.

"We'll take you there in the car. You'll save fifty yuan [seven dollars] on the bus."

Wang returns to see his family for two weeklong visits a year. Once for Chinese New Year in February, and then for the Golden Week of time off after the national holiday in October. The rest of the year, he sometimes manages to get back for a weekend when he doesn't have to work at the university, and has some money left over to make the trip. Since he started working there, for a salary of 3,000 yuan (US$425) a month, meals included, Wang has been able to go more often.

After we pass Huairou and its ultramodern village built for foreign heads of state who came for the 2014 Asia-Pacific Economic Cooperation summit, we turn off onto a narrow, winding mountain road. Wang is quick to praise the aesthetics of the luxury buildings, judging that a conference site with a view of the Great Wall improved the country's image, as well as creating jobs.

Suddenly, he looks sick. Wang is not used to traveling by car, and he rolls down the window, just in case. I figure he skipped breakfast again to save money, and feel embarrassed thinking of the buttered toast and yogurt I ate in the comfort of my apartment. Wang finally accepts my offer to ride in the front seat for the rest of the trip.

Once we pass the Great Wall, his village comes into view. Nestled in the mountains, the main street, paved with concrete, boasts a single all-purpose store, offering very little to tempt a modern consumer from Beijing. Gray, run-down houses stand in tight rows on the adjacent red laterite streets.

Wang wasn't exaggerating. With cracks running from the ground to the ceiling, his small three-room stone house lives up to its promise. The roof is about to collapse. The scruffy yard is buried in a mountain of corn stalks used to heat the place in winter. The inside walls are streaked with soot. Clothes and dishes with leftover food are scattered across the main room's concrete floor. The cardboard walls are warped to the point of falling down. The small TV set is hooked up to bare electric wires. Above the screen hangs a portrait of Mao that, every year, Wang's wife, Peng Xiuqing, religiously replaces, as the party recommends, despite the expenditure. Even in the direst poverty, the fear of being found out is omnipresent. One's faith in the party must be displayed, even if it is only through appearances.

Peng appears in a green tracksuit worn to transparency and traditional thick wool socks with holes, her hair cascading down to her ankles. Like her daughters, she has never seen the inside of a beauty salon. Her face and hands are scarlet, and she moves around painfully because of problems with her circulation. But she is proud, despite her humble conditions, and at first reluctant to speak of her family's poverty. But it turns into something like a game when it comes time for her to describe her coexistence with rats. In Beijing, for ten years, her husband's life was like that of a human rat. Meanwhile, back in his house in Yaoling, the real rodents live like kings.

"Those damn rats have taken over the house. Just look!" she declares, opening the door of the refrigerator, which is stacked with papers but without a single food item. "That's where we put our important documents because the rats haven't found a way to get inside, not yet. They've chewed up everything else."

Peng takes us on a tour of the house, pointing out the gaping holes at the base of the walls. Up to a meter (three feet) from ground level, the rodents have turned the building into a piece of Swiss cheese, going in and out as if they own the place. Ten-kilo (twenty-pound) bags of corn and rice sit on a table in the parents' room. The rats have exposed the wires for the electric blankets meant to keep the family warm, a charitable offering courtesy of the university that hired Wang. They could set the place on fire at any moment, but Peng continues to plug them in as if there were no danger.

"You can't imagine. It's just too cold in the winter," she says, throwing her arms around her body and shivering. "The children have to stay in bed. That's where they do their homework, where they eat, play, and sleep. They go weeks without warming up."

Like the parents' quarters, the children's room has a traditional Chinese bed made of stacked bricks with a plank laid on top, heated by a small stove. But the poor combustion offered by the corn stalks provides only enough heat to ward off frostbite. Laughing, the three children admit to having gotten used to the feeling of rats running across their faces while they sleep. Their faces and hands are dirty and streaked with ash. Their worn clothes have constellations of stains. A hole and a plastic pail, located behind a tarp at the rear of the yard, is their toilet, washing spot, and laundry. Cold water only. Except in winter, when the family treats itself to the luxury of a few pails of warm water so that it won't immediately freeze upon contact with the frigid air.

Wang hands me some green tea in a Pyrex cup splattered with grease and covered with filth. I take it and examine it discreetly, thinking of the rusty faucet in his kitchen. Duoyou, who hasn't forgotten our conversations about China's polluted water and its load of heavy metals that don't evaporate when it's boiled, gives me a mocking smile. I know he is waiting to see if I will drink the tea as I blow on the steaming glass. I try to reassure myself: Wang and his family are still alive. I take a few sips of the bitter liquid. Then I remember Wang's lunch invitation. The leftovers on dishes scattered on the floor and the lack of basic hygiene turn my stomach. The image of rats feasting on the house won't leave me alone. I'm practically as sick as Wang was back in the car. My mind is racing: if they have prepared a meal, how could I refuse?

I know my children won't believe me when I describe what I saw. They have been in China for a year, but how can they imagine this kind of poverty when they are living in comfort as European expatriates? Before we came here, we spent five years in Berlin. My son, Antoine, is impressed by the luxury automobiles cruising through the Beijing streets, more common here than in Germany. How can I describe the injustices inflicted on Wang's children without sounding like a propagandist for the Western way of life?

Yet Wang's three children are shining stars at school. Peng Yuxue, at seventeen, the eldest, is first in her class. Her goal was to work for the police, but that will never happen. She was very close to her objective, but an inch spoiled things for her. Yuxue is only five feet, three inches tall, and to join the police department, a person has to be at least five feet, four inches. So she will end up being a teacher. For the time being, she is trying to make up her mind between English, her favorite subject, even if she can't speak a word of it, and Chinese. Proudly, she shows off her trophies: first place in English, Chinese, and athletics, as well as collections of gifts she's received for good grades over her school career. The items remain in their plastic wrapping, like treasures.

When she considers her children's future, Peng is overcome with emotion. Her face, beauty faded from life's ordeals, is washed with tears.

"Teacher is a good job. She'll have a good salary and vacation. And she can help others who need it."

Wang is more reserved when it comes to his children's chances. When he speculates on their future, he forgets to be careful, and his bitterness about how things work in today's China takes over.

"We're too poor to be slipping envelopes to bureaucrats, professors, and university administrators. If Yuxue gets into a good university, it won't just be because of her grades. Rich people can send their kids to school even if they're dummies. Their parents just have to give an envelope to the right person. Corruption is like gangrene in this country. The poor like us are the first victims, because you need money to defend yourself. If my daughter finishes school with good grades, she'll need *guanxi* to get a job. And where there's *guanxi*, there's always money. If Mao was still around, there wouldn't be so many corrupt bureaucrats. And there wouldn't be such a big gap between rich and poor. Under Mao, we were poor and we didn't always have enough to eat, but we were all under the same roof. Today, everyone has enough to eat, but there are too many bureaucrats who can't control their appetites. Their gluttony has driven them mad. Too many have made their fortunes too fast, and people like us have been left by the wayside. Even if they're rich, the bureaucrats go on stealing from us."

His wife nods in agreement. Today's China cultivates collective amnesia. Forgotten are the disasters perpetrated by the Great Helmsman: the Great Leap Forward and its famine, the Cultural Revolution with its millions of victims ... Suddenly, realizing how careless he's been with a foreigner, Wang goes silent. On the defensive, he tells me he trusts me because he doesn't sense the usual hostility against China, even though I'm a foreigner. To gain his trust, I have refrained from criticizing the regime. My questions hold up a mirror to his own condition, though my speculations on what that might mean to him would be considered highly subversive by a party official.

After a moment of silence, Wang chimes in with a positive note. "Fortunately, I trust our president, Xi Jinping. He understands the problems. And he is fixing them through his anti-corruption campaign. He has put China back on the straight and narrow. If we hadn't had Deng Xiaoping's opening up, China's current success wouldn't have been possible. Living conditions are better. Everyone has enough to eat, and we can keep warm in winter."

Fed on the official line since she climbed out of the cradle, Yuxue rushes to back up her father. She praises the solidarity of Chinese society, pointing to a local company that paid for her schooling after the piece on her father aired on CCTV. Their neighbors donated clothing, and teachers gave the family a TV set so she could do her class presentation on a popular Chinese series, the way her classmates did.

Yuxue's face lights up when she speaks of her father. She describes the admiration she felt the day she went to visit him with her sister and brother, in his hole in the ground in Beijing. The girl had a hard time climbing down, hanging onto the walls awkwardly and slipping. Finally, she lay down in his spot. Bothered by the humidity, she had trouble breathing and didn't spend much time there. Only when she watched the show on public television did she realize how her father lived.

"I was very moved," she says. 'Until then, I didn't understand how great his sacrifices were."

All of Peng Xiuqing's self-control dissolves as she listens to her daughter, her face wet with tears.

"Wang doesn't earn much," she says, sobbing, "but he's the best of husbands and the best of fathers. Now that I can't work our plot of land because my legs hurt too much, he comes back to help out more often."

Although she is in terrible pain, Peng Xiuqing can't look after herself; she does not have the money. The little clinic in Huairou doesn't have the necessary equipment, and going to see a specialist in Beijing is beyond the couple's means.

Wang doesn't hesitate for a second when I ask him what the main problem is for the People's Republic, outside of corruption.

"China's neighbors have ambitions on our territory, and they're a real threat. We aren't strong enough yet. China must become a greater country if we want to avoid the troubles of the past."

Nationalist propaganda has done wonders. When they are not being hit by a scandal that directly touches their lives— pollution, confiscated lands, deadly cases of food poisoning—the Chinese manage to forget their real problems: the inequalities of contemporary society. The media, backed up by TV series, exploit the wounds and humiliations of the Japanese invasion during the Second World War. Suddenly, everyone is ready to sacrifice themselves for the nation.

Peng Yumei, Wang's younger daughter, age sixteen, has not yet found her vocation. His son, Peng Yushuai, fourteen, is obsessed with soccer, and this star of the local junior team dreams of becoming a professional player.

Wang did not spend more than six or seven years in school; he's not sure. He hopes his children will pursue their studies and find stable jobs.

"Before, we could not imagine any other life. But now every person in China has a dream. My dream is that our lives will be better."

◆

The day moves along quickly. With all our talk, lunchtime has come and gone. I signal to Duoyou that we should head back to Beijing if we want to make it back before dark. I can read relief in his eyes. He was in no hurry to eat in this uncomfortable shack either. I consult with him, then reach into my pocket and offer Wang some money. He refuses.

"It's my way of participating in the children's education. Take the money for them. Buy them some books," I say, putting the bills in his wife's hand. She accepts with no argument.

Then come the handshakes and hugs and promises to return. Back in the comfort of the warm car, I drop into a deep sleep after just a few bends in the road, lulled by Duoyou's smooth driving. Pursued by strange dreams, in which I see my children dressed in rags, hunted down by giant rats, I awake with a start: I am at the 3rd Ring Road. I am relieved to be back in the modern familiarity of the brightly lit towers of the Beijing Central Business District.

CHAPTER 4

RETIREMENT IN JULONG GARDEN

"**N**ew York is finished. Beijing is going to be the next center of the world," I told my daughter, Joséphine, trying to convince her to come with me to China back in 2013.

In the underground chambers beneath Julong (Dragon) Garden, our apartment building, we discovered dormitories filled with *mingong*. Most of them are married, but only those who work in maintenance in the building live as couples. The rest are sentenced to celibacy. The men, with black faces, work on nearby construction sites. The women, with dark circles under their eyes, clean the restaurants and bars around the Workers' Stadium (Gongti). Their shift on the surface runs from eleven a.m. to five p.m., then nine p.m. to six a.m. The rest of the time, they disappear under the ground.

Like most people who live in Julong Garden, we had no idea that a parallel universe existed beneath our feet, a few steps from the hippest nightclubs in China—in all Asia, for that matter—that graced our district. Dazzled by the modern face of Beijing, the superficial easy freedom that made it possible for her to hang out with her friends in nightspots whose doors would be barred to her back home, Joséphine could hardly imagine that a shadow world had sprung up right below our apartment. It took us a year to discover it—thanks to my research. China is a country of violent contradictions, where appearances can be deceiving. If you dig a little deeper, you often encounter a different reality, the exact opposite of the first. My predecessor at the newspaper's office, Jean Leclerc du Sablon, who was passionate about the People's Republic and closely followed its evolution since the economic reforms, used to call the country the Empire of Smoke and Mirrors. Nothing much has changed.

"You're right, it's like New York here," Joséphine said, after descending into the entrails of Beijing with me. "It's like the immigrants arriving at Ellis Island at the end of the nineteenth century—the very bottom of the barrel—and the poverty they had to endure to attain the American dream. The difference is that we don't know what the Chinese dream is. We don't even know if it exists."

She might have been pushing the comparison, but it's true: China's complexity can be destabilizing. The syndrome has struck me, too. One day's certainties and the feeling that you've finally understood something about the country can be swept aside by another reality and another viewpoint the next. One day, I am impressed by the success of a billionaire open to Western ideas; or the intelligence, curiosity, and English-language skills of young model students from Shanghai, the best in the world; or by the yearning for prosperity of the Chinese middle classes, whose desire for comfort seems to have pushed aside their political aspirations. The next day, I am shocked by the violent inequalities judged as a temporary but necessary evil by the Communist Party that reigns unchallenged over the country. Conversations with peasants whose land has been expropriated for the profit of promoters on a first-name basis with corrupt local party officials, or with Chinese economists who state that the level of development will stagnate without democratic reforms, awaken new doubts. As I get to know the rat tribe, those doubts are reinforced. Aren't the rats the coolies of modern China? Their fate is a powerful warning that shakes even the most Sino-optimistic certainties about the potential for China's economic development and advancement.

◆

It's a sure thing: the mixture of incredulity and discomfort that arises when, with the tone of a tour guide, I inform the non-Chinese residents of Julong Garden that a shadowy underground world exists beneath their luxury apartments.

"Where are those rats of yours?" a neighbor asks me in a mocking tone. "We never see them."

Another woman peppers me with questions: "Where do those people come from? What are they doing down there? How do they live? Do they have kitchens and bathrooms?"

A woman from France who lives in a nearby building taken over by foreigners asks me to organize a tour to see the strange wonders hidden in my basement. She wants to discover the unseen side of Beijing. Taken aback, I answer a little harshly—"Of course, I'll bring along some peanuts so you can feed them. It'll be just like the zoo"—and am rewarded with an embarrassed smile.

A button in the elevator: that is all that separates our daily life—our re-creation of Western comfort with a dash of Chinese exoticism—from the world of the living dead. The dragon of Julong lost its luster a long time ago. Touted as a "luxury residence" by real estate agencies, Julong Garden possesses all the grace of a low-rent housing project from the 1970s. The rats' entrance can be found in Building 7. On the upper floors is the local Greenpeace chapter, and on the second level, offices of foreign media and an investors' club. The B2 button takes visitors downstairs, where the elevator doors open onto a room whose tiles have turned off-white. The light is spectral and wavering. An old black sofa covered in dust sits to one side with boxes piled on it. At first glance, there seems to be no human presence, but soon you spot wires strung in corners to dry clothes: underwear, socks, shirts, and pants. Street clothes are mixed in with uniforms: the blue and gray blouses of the *ayi* who do the cleaning, a waiter's outfit, the blue overalls worn by workers ... The display of the underpaid professions of big Chinese cities is virtually complete.

Some forty *mingong* are crammed into a large dim dormitory with a concrete floor. Fifteen women work in a nightclub in the Workers' Stadium, where the glittering society of hip Beijing hangs out; they rent their common lodging from their boss. Lined up against the walls, their metal bunk beds fill the room. In a room at the end of a hallway, the owner of a neighboring restaurant has put up a dozen employees. The cost of rent in the center of town, as well as the need to find lodgings close to work, so that they can face their demanding shifts without long commutes, have forced people to accept these appalling conditions. A sickly-sweet odor grows sharper as we near the bathroom. A single facility for both sexes, with no lighting and one entrance, separated by a small partition, with two sinks for the entire group. On the women's side, four individual stalls. On the men's, four urinals and three squat toilets send up a powerful smell. No shower, no hot water.

Each of the seventy people who rent space here makes do with a plastic basin, and the water comes from a faucet in the bathroom.

After a half hour down here, Duoyou feels the same thing I do: a powerful desire to get to the surface and breathe some fresh air. Outside, even at a pollution level that would cause urban centers in Western cities to be closed, the air feels almost clear compared to the atmosphere underground.

At the end of a hallway, an unexpected encounter stops us in our tracks.

"You've gotten lost! I've never seen a renter from upstairs down here," exclaims Zheng Yuanchao with a big smile. He is the caretaker who picks up the garbage and looks after maintenance in our unit. "Not even a Chinese resident would come down here. I never thought I'd run into a *laowai*."

A charming older gentleman from Hubei province, Zheng never fails to greet the *laowai* he meets along the pathways of Julong with a warm, openhearted *nihao*. This makes a pleasant contrast to the usual Beijing manners. In the months after we first settled in the city, his benevolent smile was a comfort as we navigated our way through this giant overpopulated megacity. I owe him an explanation.

"I'm doing research for a book about the people who live underground in Beijing," I tell him, hoping the subject won't alarm him. My previous experience has taught me that revealing my intentions so directly can provoke a wall of silence.

I push on. "I didn't think that people lived under the ground in Julong, too. I discovered a labyrinth here. This place is completely incredible. Are the storage lockers here, too?"

Mr Zheng places one thumb up to show he approves of my joke. "*Hao, hao, hao*! A very good subject. When people talk about Beijing, everyone wants to know about the big successes, the glass towers, the money, the fancy cars. No one talks about life beneath the ground."

"Do you live here? Can you show me around?"

"Wait, here's my wife." He turns to her. "This man is a famous writer," he informs her, though he has no idea whether I have any more skill than the average journalist. "He's writing about people who live down below. He wants to see how we do it."

His wife, Liu Shuzen, shares maintenance responsibilities in our building with her husband. She wears a doubtful look, and I can feel that my presence has caused feelings of incredulity, mixed with concern. In the end, the couple invites me into the kitchen. It is getting close to dinnertime, and the Chinese don't skimp on hospitality, even when they live at the bottom of a pit. At the end of a hallway, to the right, a door closed off by a heavy metal grille gives onto the garage. Well lit by fluorescent tubes, immaculate parking spaces are occupied by Mercedes and Audis and the odd Porsche—the property of rich owners up above. On the left, a dim concrete stairway gives the underground inhabitants access to the kitchens of the first-level basement. Another small hallway with four successive kitchen facilities borders the garage. The exhaust pipes of luxury cars sending out toxic emissions add to the atmosphere. Employed by Julong management, three senior couples in charge of maintenance each have their personal spot where they can store their belongings and make their meals. It is Chinese New Year, and the menu is traditional: *jiaozi*, boiled dumplings. The only variation is the stuffing: pork and carrots, or pork and spinach.

"We have a visitor. A famous writer!" Zheng announces, maintaining an air of mystery that is both advantageous to us and beneficial to his image. Whatever their social status, the Chinese share the same obsession with playing host.

Welcoming a foreign guest is considered an honor, but letting a journalist run free in the kitchen is more like a calamity. Luckily, Zheng's warm welcome calms his wary neighbors. Coming from the four corners of a country as big as a continent, the families know the art of living in conditions that would discourage anyone else. The kitchens are not what most would call clean, and they have no running water, ventilation, or refrigeration. But through their warmth and community spirit, they communicate something noble, and that feeling fills the kitchen and cancels out the fatigue of their harsh existence, and makes this little celebration possible. The smells of cooking and the heady spices that flavor the dumplings have a further use: they cover up the odor of urine and excrement mixed with detergent that clings to the walls of the underground passages. Standing in front of a meat grinder on a wooden block, the men mix the stuffing, while at a miniature Formica table, the women place the stuffing in the middle of the dough with their chopsticks, and then seal each dumpling with an expert touch. Then they drop them into boiling water in woks set on top of hot plates. Once they're cooked, the *jiaozi* are set on a common platter. Everyone serves themselves, dipping the food into a little bowl filled with a mix of vinegar and soy sauce, spiced with finely chopped red chili.

◆

I had to wait for another meeting to get down to brass tacks with Zheng. A few weeks went by before he agreed to reveal his secrets. We set up a first interview on a Saturday afternoon, when his workload was not as heavy, but at the appointed hour, Zheng was nowhere to be found. The old man claimed he had forgotten, then admitted that his enthusiasm for our project had tapered off. He did not want his name appearing in the book in case it was translated into Chinese, a most unlikely scenario, given the party's devoted censors. When journalists escape the vigilance of the state security apparatus that is continually trying to keep us from investigating "sensitive" subjects, a second safety net—the censors—makes sure the masses will have no access to information considered subversive in the eyes of the party.

In the end, Zheng agrees to speak to us after we offer to hide him and his wife behind pseudonyms.

"In that case, you're on. You can call me Zheng Yuanchao and my wife will be Liu Shuzen."

"Are these people you want to get into trouble, or the heroes of your favorite TV show?" I ask, a little surprised by his ready-made reply.

"No, no, just names we've always liked," Zheng answers, laughing.

At age sixty-two, he has been retired for two years. He worked in a factory, building barges for river transport in Wuhan, the capital of Hubei province, for Dongfeng, a company known worldwide for its associations with car makers. In 1974, he joined the People's Liberation Army as a private serving the officers. He was demobilized in 1980, when Deng Xiaoping decided to reduce the ranks of unnecessary soldiers. He joined the factory then and retired in the summer of 2013. Meanwhile, his wife, age sixty-three, a peasant, grew vegetables on her little *mu* of land, 806.65 square yards (0.165 acre), and sold them at the market. Zheng admits they could have lived—more like survived—in their village of Huangang, near Wuhan, continuing to cultivate their parcel of land to feed themselves and supplement their income, as well as Zheng's pension. But that did not work out because of their two sons, twenty-six and twenty-seven years old. Both of them found jobs and are financially independent. One is a barber in Wuhan, and the other earned a diploma in mechanical engineering and repairs the enormous bulldozers used in construction projects in the southern province of Yunnan. But neither has married. Their parents went to work in Beijing to pay for their dowries. In the Chinese tradition, the future husband must give an apartment, jewelry, or money, sometimes even a car, to his wife-to-be. Without the promise of basic material comfort for the fiancée, marriage is unthinkable.

"In Huangang, you have to buy an apartment for the bride and give her 200,000 yuan [US$28,500]," Zheng complains. "In China, you don't marry a woman, you buy her."

He and his wife have put some money aside, but they will have to work many more long years to amass the 400,000 yuan (US$57,000) needed to purchase apartments for their two sons. Zheng looks half-dead, with the dark circles under his eyes, and admits that it's hard for him, tolerating this life of city rats, when he has a house in the countryside in his native village, where the air is clean.

"At the beginning, I couldn't breathe in our room," he says. "And I had headaches because of the bad smells. My wife didn't do any better. But her work in the apartment building is easier than what she did in the fields."

Liu does her best to keep up a certain elegance. Her hair is twisted into a single, long braid, and she wears a short, Chinese-style jacket over a white blouse. Her face is astonishingly fresh for a woman living beneath the ground. Whereas, unshaven and disheveled, Zheng puts on the same pair of worn pants and camouflage army jacket every day. The couple dreamed of life in Beijing before they actually arrived here, but now, suffering from pollution and the poverty, they haven't had the courage or the means to visit the Forbidden City, the Great Wall, or the Temple of Heaven, the way they promised themselves they would.

"You have to pay to get in. It's too expensive for us," Zheng reports. "All we saw was Tiananmen Square. Beijing isn't as good as I thought it would be. The air is rotten with pollution. The people look down on us because we're from the country, and they're impolite. They throw their cigarette butts everywhere and spit on the ground. And what they call cooking ... To tell the truth, people are a lot more civilized in our village."

Their children face the humiliation of not being able to marry, but do they not feel equivalent shame at seeing their parents slaving away for pennies and living underground?

"They visited us only once in two years. It's hard for them to see how we live," Zheng admits. "They pity us, but they know we don't have a choice."

My own children ended up getting interested in the fate of the human rats. My research has given them a different view of the city, a contrast to what they see on the surface, the scrubbed appearance of their daily life. My daughter's expeditions to night-clubs where the gilded youth of Beijing hang out, and the lunches my son shares with his friends at the American and Mexican restaurants, have taught them nothing about the country's social realities. Very few expat children are familiar with local problems. They are too surrounded by the modern world of city centers, with multiplex movie houses and restaurants, lounges, and nightclubs that are as chic as anything in Paris, New York, or Berlin, all at cheap prices and accessible to teenagers. In the evenings, Antoine and Joséphine can't get enough of my stories of the underground. For them, they sound like something out of the Middle Ages.

"Those people are completely crazy to sacrifice themselves for their kids!" declares Antoine, age fourteen. "And their kids! How can they do that to their parents? Don't they care? Don't worry, we'd never make you do anything like that."

"Oh, don't worry, that will never happen," my wife jokes.

◆

Between the two of them, Zheng Yuanchao and Liu Shuzen earn a monthly salary of 3,000 (US$425) yuan at Julong Garden, plus 1,800 yuan (US$250) for Zheng's pension. At 4,800 yuan (US$675) a month, they have long years of labor ahead of them. But they suspect that their residency at Julong will soon be coming to an end.

"The management is going to fire us," Liu predicts with the resigned look of someone who accepts their fate. "They hire old people to do the maintenance because they can pay them less than younger ones, and they can put us up in bad conditions. If we're not happy, they tell us to seek our fortune elsewhere, because they know very well that a retired person doesn't have much chance of finding another job. But we can't get too old, or work here too long, because they're afraid they'll have to pay our medical costs if we get sick or have an accident."

The *mingong* often have no health insurance, which creates a moral responsibility for their employers to pay those costs. Zheng and Liu intend to go back to their village after they are let go. She will go back to the fields and he will try to find work in a factory.

"It won't be any worse, even if it won't be easy to find something at my age," Zheng says. "Here, we have lost our freedom."

Will China offer their two sons a better future?

"It depends on them," he says prudently. "Today, in China, everything is possible. The central government's policies are good, even if too many bureaucrats at the local level are corrupt. But the state has to protect the poor better. Because the rich are getting richer while the poor stay poor."

Zheng and Liu share a dormitory in the second-level basement with three other couples who work maintenance in the apartment complex. An entranceway equipped with a television and a few chairs serves as their common room. Metal cupboards contain their personal effects, and separate the 20-square-meter

(215-square-foot) space into four tiny rooms furnished with a bunk bed and a small night table. The place is hardly a haven of privacy. When the woman on the next bed is watching her favorite TV series, cranking up the volume because of her hearing problems and laughing uproariously every time her hero lets fly with a clever word, the three other couples have no choice but to participate.

One of their neighbors, a short, stocky man with a bald head and powerful hands, who chain-smokes despite the wisdom of his sixty-two years, arrived a couple of years ago from his village of Weidong, in Heilongjiang province, where he grew corn. He has a small monthly pension of 800 yuan (US$115), since he paid into the peasants' credit union, but his wife receives nothing. The couple owns a small house on their land, but they came to Beijing to work and save money so as to not depend on their children.

"We don't want to be a burden for our kids. We're managing to put aside 30,000 yuan [US$4,300] a year," he reports. "But I don't know how much longer they'll keep us on here. And if we have a serious problem with our health, our money won't go far."

"You're really out to destroy the myth of the retired Chinese person who travels abroad and spends his money on presents to bring back," we joke.

"Travel abroad?" The retired peasant bursts out laughing. "I never even dreamed of it. I don't even have enough to visit the Forbidden City. But my son has a good job in computers and maybe he'll be able to retire one day."

Many people are forced to work after retirement age because of the very small pensions. And the problem shows no signs of improving. China may well get old before getting rich. The most populous country on earth is facing a rapidly aging populace, made worse by the effects of the one-child policy, which has created a shortage of young workers to replace the old ones. The country will have to get to work on that problem before focusing on other emerging economies. The government is preparing to reform the pension system and will have to increase the retirement age for the first time in fifty years. It took until 2017 to unveil a detailed reform package, because of "a lack of social consensus on the issue," despite what the experts, who are unanimous, say: the situation is urgent.

"Why wait five years to make a plan, and another five to put it into action?" wonders Yao Yang, a professor at Peking University. "In 2022, the pension system deficit will be an enormous problem. We need to apply progressive reforms immediately, since the baby boomer generation is reaching retirement age, and there are a lot of them."

In Beijing, many retired people, like Zheng and Liu, work for starvation wages. The intersection in front of the Wumart department store in Beiqijia, a northern suburb of Beijing, and one of the hiring points for illegal day laborers, practically turns into a riot every time a vehicle slows down. With their experienced eye, veteran *mingong* swoop down like birds fighting for breadcrumbs. A potential employer slides his electric window down, attracting a cloud of candidates in their blue workers' uniforms, then speeds off after taking on a heavyset guy in his thirties. Dozens of men in their sixties retreat to the sidewalk, but their determination remains fierce. Finding work to add to their meager pension is a matter of life and death.

Sharp-eyed and fleet-footed, Ding Weiguo, age sixty, and Zhao Huatian, fifty-nine, put on an acrobatic show to display their excellent shape. This pair of old comrades has all the comic possibilities of a Laurel and Hardy show, Chinese-style.

"I come here every morning at six, because there's no way I can survive on my pension—seventy yuan [ten dollars] a month. That's not even enough to buy a handful of vegetables," Ding Weiguo points out. He carries his drill and other tools over his shoulder like a sling, as well as a kit bag in case he's called upon to sleep at a construction site. "Yesterday, I got an electrician's job. I made 150 yuan [US$20] in one day." A native of nearby Hebei province, where he once worked the land, Ding settled in the capital a few months back, after reaching retirement age. He shares an underground room with another pensioner from Hebei for 300 yuan (US$40) a month. His wife stayed behind in the village, where she keeps working the land. "I can save 800 to 1,000 yuan [US$115–140] a month, and I send her the money so she can live," he reports. "I was with her for three weeks in February for the new year. And I'll go back in October for the harvest. I'll keep doing that as long as I'm physically able."

Ding's friend Zhao Huatian is not as fortunate. He has never received his pension. Wearing a straw hat to protect against the sun's early rays, Zhao explains, "To get it, you have to be on good terms with the village party secretary, and he's corrupt. Some people get their pension at forty-five." But Zhao never considered complaining. "The party guys all stick together," he accuses. "You want them to send the police to my house and harass my family?"

Zhao has no skills when it comes to electricity or the building trades, and this simple farmer from Hebei hasn't worked in four days. "The last time a guy hired me, it was to carry bricks all day. Tough work, all for 80 yuan [US$11.50], and I hurt like hell in the evening," he remembers with a rueful smile. "The bosses want young men, but if you manage to work once or twice for the same one, you can win him over by showing you're up for anything."

When the day comes when they're not strong enough to work, Zhao and Ding will have to depend on their sons to take them in, according to Chinese tradition. But their sons are migrants, too, leaving their wives and children in the village to find jobs in Beijing. They can hardly make ends meet.

"We'll go and live with our daughters-in-law," the two unfortunate grandfathers admit. "But not until our bodies give out. The day we can't pass out those red envelopes with a 100-yuan [15 dollars] note inside at weddings and funerals in the village, that'll be like we're dead already."

According to estimates by the United Nations, approximately one-quarter of the population will be over sixty by the year 2030. The senior population is growing so rapidly in China that their children have no way of taking care of them, despite Chinese tradition dictating that elderly parents are their responsibility. This graying of society, combined with the effects of the one-child policy, is weighing heavily on the country, reducing the workforce and leaving the younger generation to look after their parents on their own, without siblings to share the load.

In the 1950s, after the civil war, when life expectancy was less than forty-five, the leaders of the Communist Party, who had just taken over, judged it reasonable to set the retirement age relatively young. But now that life expectancy for men is seventy-two and seventy-seven for women, the average age of retirement of fifty-three doesn't make sense. Officially, retirement can be taken at sixty for men, and some women can stop working as early as fifty. To make things worse, the active population between sixteen and fifty-nine has dropped off since 2012: 67 percent of the overall population, compared to 69.2 percent in 2010. In 2015, the ratio of working people needed to finance a retired person was 3.04 to 1. By 2050, it will fall to 1.3 to 1, according to official statistics. The government is planning to gradually raise retirement ages over the years so that retirement age for both men and women is sixty-five by 2045. The government is also aiming to increase workers' contributions to their pensions.

In the center of Beijing, the happy urban retirees of Ditan Park provide a stark contrast with the pensioners from the countryside. In the cities, the minimum pension level is set at 2,000 yuan (US$285) a month, whereas it stands at 55 (US$8) in rural areas. Accompanied by a group of musicians, grandmothers belt out traditional folk tunes, while others practice Tai Chi or play with their grandchildren. Former high officials, skilled at calligraphy, draw characters on the ground with a water-soaked brush. Another group of men meet up with their birds, carried in bamboo cages, ready to sing.

The pleasant facade hides a precarious reality. Hanging from metal bars, a group of sixty-somethings does monkey imitations with Olympic prowess.

"My medical costs aren't covered. If something happens, I'll have to pay. So I better stay in shape," a former party official tells me as he jumps to the ground.

Despite his gray hair, he bounces right back up, almost as flexible as a young man. He once worked for a state company, and now he owns his apartment, and receives 3,000 yuan (US$425) a month to provide a decent living. Decent—but no more.

"If I get really sick, it's a death sentence. I won't be able to pay. So I take care of myself," he repeats, and admits he can only dream of the pensions paid in "the developed nations." His idea of the West may be a bit rosier than the reality.

CHAPTER 5

CHINESE WOMEN ON THE VERGE OF A NERVOUS BREAKDOWN

Adorable in her little flowered dress, the girl bites into an apple and glances around, blasé. Meanwhile, her mother urges her forward. The woman is a Gong Li look-alike, right down to the careful makeup and all the trinkets of the new Chinese middle class, including the Louis Vuitton bag, black slacks, white silk blouse, and latest smartphone. The girl, ten years old at the most, is late for her piano lesson. At seven on a Friday evening, the girl's week is far from over. Every night, after a quick hour of playtime and dinner, she attends private lessons until eleven. Under the thin Communist veneer displayed out of obligation, and then only in public and without enthusiasm, just to avoid trouble, Confucian values have made a triumphant return among the middle class.

According to the Confucian tradition deeply ingrained in Chinese society, it is possible to succeed in everything, including changing your destiny, through hard work. The will to succeed is inculcated in children by their parents, whose ambitions are centered on their only heir, who must bear the burden alone of honorably carrying on the family name, because of the one-child policy. At school, teachers are so respected that asking them a question is unthinkable; it would be like suggesting the lesson plan was imperfect. Outside of school, the children spend their weekends doing homework, playing in chess tournaments, studying their best subjects in accelerated courses paid for by their parents, experimenting in chemistry labs, and boning up on their physics or calligraphy. In my house, the very mention of the thirst for knowledge and the success of children in model Chinese schools makes my son and daughter burst out in sighs of exasperation. In China, education is the key to mobility and advancement, the very opposite of the forced migration of the rat people.

"My daughter takes private math lessons three times a week. It makes her mind more agile," her mother declares proudly. "She's taking English classes, too, three times weekly, so she can explore the world. Soon, she will be able to surf online sites in English, and later, study abroad. We won't wait for her to reach university. When she turns fourteen, we'll send her to a college in London, so she can learn their ways, and the doors to the best British universities will open to her."

The prestige of English universities is not the only motivation for moneyed parents in Beijing. Preparing an exit strategy for their children in case the People's Republic doesn't evolve in favorable fashion is one of the priorities of the middle class. Pollution, contaminated food scandals, endemic corruption, the domination of the party, suppressed freedom, spying on the internet—the hazards of modern China are many. As it becomes the world's premier economic power, the People's Republic will always need executives trained in Western methods in foreign universities. Chinese people with diplomas from Oxford and Cambridge will have no trouble making careers for themselves in overseas multinationals if things turn sour back home.

"On the weekend, she goes to dance classes and participates in math contests. She's training for the math Olympics," her mother says, very seriously.

Every year, all the big cities in China organize contests classified by age in an array of disciplines: chess, badminton, chemistry, math ... At the end of their schooling, the national champions are named—their first step in a life of success. Generally, when I talk about Chinese education and the progress in the big-city schools, my Western friends laugh. They believe their system is superior. They criticize rote learning, which leads to a lack of creative thinking that will sink Chinese students, not to mention the strict discipline. Some of this criticism may be warranted, but my friends have lost sight of one essential thing: the Chinese yearn for success and trust in a brighter future.

The charming woman in her forties glances at her watch.

"We've done it again. We're going to be late for her piano lesson. Bye-bye!" she calls, waving in my direction.

Despite her stiletto heels, she sets off running. She roughly grabs her daughter by the arm, dragging her behind, and the little girl drops her apple after only a couple bites. No time to go back and pick it up. Two women are sitting on benches along the walkway that separates two buildings. They have witnessed the scene, and they keep their eyes on the apple, looking at the mother and daughter moving away, and casting eyes on each other. The dark gray sky is turning black, heavy with pollution, mosquitoes, and electricity, about to break open. For the inhabitants of ground-level Beijing, it is the sign that a downpour is about to wash the sky and the city streets. For those who live in its underbelly, it announces the upcoming battle against the flood of liquid pollution about to wash into their living quarters.

The women's worn faces and unfashionable clothes that have seen better days speak of where they come from. Unlike the mother and her child, they have nothing to do with the above-level apartments that belong to the Beijing middle class. Instead, they are part of the underground world of the *shuzu*, the rat tribe. Now that the elegant mother and child have moved off, the quickest will triumph. Shuying gets to her feet and pounces on the apple. In a show of sour grapes, the other woman looks away, acting as though she never had any interest in the degrading competition. Shuying displays no embarrassment, wiping off the green apple with her hands and biting into it. Three-quarters of it was left, and it takes her only a minute or two to finish it off, down to the core, nothing left but the seeds, which she holds between her teeth, then spits out. She'll throw the stem into the bushes after chewing on it a while.

◆

By order of the central party authorities, the local propagandists used the walls of Xibahe Zhongli, the middle-class residential development along the 3rd Ring Road, in the heart of Beijing, to post a giant portrait of Lei Feng. This model hero, the Communist fetish of Maoist propaganda, was presented as the example to follow for all Chinese people, no matter their age, starting in the 1960s. Since then, he has made regular appearances whenever ideological discipline calls for it. He regained pride of place under President Xi Jinping's campaign for a return to Maoist values, which was supposed to fight the increasing influence of universal values. For the Chinese leader, freedom, human rights, democracy, and the multiparty system are no more than weapons used by Western countries to weaken China.

Lei Feng, whose real existence is open to question, was supposed to have joined the People's Liberation Army in 1960, before his untimely death in August 1962 at age twenty-one, when he was crushed by a falling telephone pole. The propagandists' imaginations turned Lei Feng, always humble and at the service of the people, into an invincible protector of borders, a Stakhanov-style worker breaking all records of coal production, an ideal comrade who would awake in the night to wash his roommates' socks, and most of all, an assiduous reader of the Little Red Book who learned the quotations of Chairman Mao by heart.

"Learn the spirit of Lei Feng. Be a civilized and polite citizen of Beijing," the slogan beneath the portrait advises.

Next to him, a second giant party mural shows the Great Wall and reminds the residents of Xibahe Zhongli of the core socialist values: prosperity, democracy, freedom, equality, rule of law, patriotism, dedication, integrity, friendship ... The people who live on the surface and those in the underground share few things, but they are united in their indifference toward party slogans.

Once night falls, the rat people of Xibahe Zhongli slip down the concrete stairways that lead to the entrails of the building, leaping from one stone to the next to keep from getting their feet wet, along the passageways bathed in brackish water. They disappear into their hutches hidden behind curtains and doorways. The way down to their refuge is around the back of Building 5. The tribe has occupied all of the underground that lies beneath the feet of middle-class families. With no daylight, the *shuzu* of Xibahe Zhongli depend on buzzing fluorescent tubes. They breathe stinking, overheated air, saturated with moisture and mosquitoes. The tiles of the halls are sticky, and rainwater from summer storms flows through the communal kitchen and toilets, then spreads across the common areas and into people's rooms.

The propaganda messages have reached all the way down to the subterranean passageways. Posters displaying modern parking garages and immaculate hallways line the crumbling walls of this cavernous world, with slogans in perfect contradiction to reality, a sort of absurdist party exercise that no one believes in, as if the inhabitants had put them up with ironic intent: "Build harmony in Beijing basements," or "Underground spaces must satisfy the non-profit works of society," and, with total sincerity, "Underground areas belong to reserve military infrastructures. Renting subterranean rooms is forbidden."

"How can anyone survive in such unhealthy and abject conditions? The place is completely unlivable," said Élise, the intern who accompanied me the first time I went exploring.

Life underground exposes the rat people to a host of disorders: psychological problems, anxiety, depression, skin diseases, and respiratory ailments.

"It's no place to raise a child," declares Xinyu, age twenty-three, as she slips on a windbreaker inspired by the colors of the Chinese national Olympic team. She is going out with her twenty-month-old daughter, who is already running toward the exit. "In our village, in Anhui, we have a big house and all the fresh air we can breathe. Here, my daughter has only one thing on her mind, and that's to get out, to breathe the air and see the sunshine."

A poster down another hallway seems to be a comical comment on life underground, since its messages are in complete contradiction to the subterranean reality, except for the safety issues. "Do not block the exit. Do not install windows or doors at the exits. Do not leave large objects in front of the exits and stairways. Prohibited: the use of hot plates, electric radiators, power bars." Illustrations showing a burned-out television and air-conditioning unit serve as stark warnings. Other photos display submerged cars in the parking garage, with a reminder of the rules: "During heavy rains, the rescue teams must act quickly to block access to the garage and basements. People must be evacuated."

Accidents happen frequently in these unfit spaces. But like with highway deaths, suicides, wealthy people moving overseas, and the number of imprisoned dissidents and journalists, the government publishes no official statistics or complete figures on the number of deaths by drowning or fire in the Beijing underground. Like other authoritarian regimes, the party is allergic to sensitive information that reveals society's true state. Yet Chinese media often report on deaths by drowning or fire in subterranean Beijing, but this does not prevent the inhabitants from cooking on small hot plates in the hallways, or plugging in a number of appliances with bare wires into old, overloaded power bars, or heating in winter with extra radiators that resemble slowly ticking incendiary devices. I can't help thinking of those factories that explode on a regular basis in this country, killing hundreds of workers, since safety standards are not respected. The lives of the working class are not valued in China. The pressure for profit above all else, the backroom deals and corruption that make it easy to break the rules, lead to large-scale catastrophes in this biggest of nations. The intense summer rains cause numerous deaths, and when the water rises as the rat tribe sleeps, the results are often fatal. The stairways to safety are frequently turned into communal storehouses, loaded down with furniture. The handrails are studded with hangers, so as to serve as closets. The steps are littered with people's shoes. No better trap could be laid.

"Do you have a plan in case of a flood?" we ask.

"We have never had a death by drowning in our basement," says a shoe vendor proudly. The man, originally from Shandong province, has been living here for ten years. "When it rains, we fill sandbags and put them in front of the entrances and the ramp to the parking garage, and that keeps the water from rushing in. It's a battle of wills, and we all work together. It can take us all night when it really starts raining."

So far, their mobilization has kept catastrophe at bay. Although they have escaped flooding, the underground inhabitants have to face leaks. During rainy periods, up to an inch of water can cover the floor. A viscous coating composed of the dirt the water carries, mixed with the grime from shoes, and the filth from backed-up sinks and toilets turns the surfaces into a skating rink. This stinking, damp magma suits insects just fine, and they lay their eggs in it.

"Do the people who live above ever help out?"

A look of consternation greets our question. The man from Shandong, solidly built, hair dyed black, has all the accoutrements of a prosperous small business owner, with his iPhone attached to his belt, his jeans, and his brand-name sneakers. He has yet to decide whether we are dangerous morons who will get him in trouble with the authorities or mean-spirited gawkers who have come to laugh in his face.

"And what about the teachings of Lei Feng? Didn't he say we must serve the people?" we push further, with a benevolent smile.

That does it! We have made our way down here to torture him with our dubious political jokes. With a thin smile, the shoe vendor turns on his heel, then closes the thick orange curtain of his door in our faces and launches into an agitated discussion with his daughter. She was watching us, suspicion in her eyes, from the hallway.

Discouraged, we are about to give up when we cross paths with Shuying again. Our first meeting with her dates back to summer 2014—our very first contact with the rat people, our first descent into Beijing's subterranean maze. We passed ourselves off as sociologists in order to not be escorted out the door immediately, but we didn't last two hours. A drunk inhabitant expelled us forcefully, loudly calling down his wrath on us and his neighbors. We had no choice but to retreat, slipping away shamefacedly.

At the time, Shuying, age thirty-nine, was a cleaning woman who had been in Beijing for six months. She couldn't hold back her tears as she spoke of her fifteen-year-old daughter and seven-year-old son who had stayed behind in their village in Shandong province.

"We'll have to get used to this life." She sighed, then added, "We're making these sacrifices to give them a better future. I don't want our kids to have to live like us, like rats. My daughter wants to be a Chinese professor and we hope to pay for her studies. That's why we came to Beijing to work."

Her husband found a job as a garbage collector. They couldn't do better than this eight-square-meter (eighty-six-square-foot) hutch with a rudimentary kitchen area with a gas heater and no opening to the outside. Rent: 650 yuan (US$90). Attached to the ceiling, the clothesline, on which the couple's entire wardrobe hung, formed a complex spiderweb. The day we visited, the employees of the offices she cleaned had given her two boxed meals that had hardly been touched. The dinner was most welcome, since she and her husband barely had enough to get by.

I had warned my intern Élise that Shuying would probably break down when questioned about her children, but she was shaken by her reaction all the same.

"That is the difficult part of our job," I told Élise. "Sometimes we know that a certain question will bring tears, but we ask it anyway."

"How can anyone live like that?" Élise wondered, whispering so that Duoyou could still hear Shuying's answer. "It's inhuman. I know it's not the worst part, but it's terrible to hear her say how happy she was to be able to bring back a couple half-eaten trays of food so they could have dinner. I'd be so humiliated."

Shuying smiled and pointed to two spare mattresses leaning against the wall. The humiliation wasn't over.

"I'm so happy," she confided. "The kids will be coming next week for summer vacation."

Things are different now, on this day. The degrading scene with the apple that we witnessed, the way we were thrown out, the neighbors' criticism ... Shuying is trying to avoid us.

"Do you remember us?" we ask awkwardly.

She nods her head, embarrassed, then heads for her lodgings, and safety.

"I'm writing a book about people living underground, like you, who have come from the countryside. I wanted to see how you are, and find out how you're adapting to this life."

I haven't quite convinced her. Not at all. She has retreated to her room and is about to close the door in our faces. One last chance.

"I remember that your daughter wanted to be a teacher."

"Ah, so you remember that." Shuying's face lights up. She invites us in.

"I promise, we will be more careful today. We won't make you cry," we say, to try to lighten the atmosphere.

Her hair pulled back with a rubber band, she acknowledges us with a smile. Emotion has colored her cheeks. In her pale pink jacket and white lace collar over a pair of black slacks, Shuying displays a certain elegance. Of course, living beneath the ground hasn't done her much good. Over the last year, her face has taken on new lines and her hair has gone white. Neither Duoyou nor I recognized her at first.

Shuying has a new job, and in the evening she feels the demands it makes on her body. She works from five a.m. to one p.m. in a school cafeteria where she makes meals for the children. In the afternoons, she cleans private apartments in a nearby building. She doesn't make it home until seven p.m. When the air outside is breathable, she will sit on a bench by her "rathole," relaxing and catching her breath before heading down below.

"At first I couldn't breathe in that tiny dank room," she says. "I was anxious and depressed. In my village, near the city of Zaozhuang [some 600 kilometers, or 375 miles, south of Beijing], I had a big two-story house. It took me a few months to get used to this room."

Shuying never complains about her life when her husband is around. His is even more demanding. He drives a street sweeper from eight a.m. to seven p.m., then moves on to a second job, as night watchman in an apartment block, from eight p.m. to midnight.

"Every evening, when he comes back, he's exhausted." She sighs. "But there's no choice. The money he makes will help pay for our daughter's studies. Back in the village, he drove a little truck that carried sand and freight, but our income wasn't enough to see to our children's futures. I worked in the fields until the government confiscated the land. That was five years ago. They gave me financial compensation, and that helped us build the house, but there was no work for me in the region and we couldn't make a decent living."

I shiver when I consider that her current life seems less harsh than what she knew back in her village. People from Shandong, a province with a stormy history, have a reputation for being tough and resilient. In 1938, the province was invaded by the Japanese imperial army. In 1942, General Yasuji Okamura instituted the scorched earth Three Alls Policy (kill all, burn all, loot all). During the Great Leap Forward, from 1958 to 1963, the region suffered from the famine more than the rest of China, and cases of cannibalism were reported. But Shandong is also the former state of Lu, where Confucius lived and died.

Shuying believes she can change her fate, and her children's fate, through hard work. At the same time, she is not afraid to criticize the squalor in which she lives, as she chops away at a piece of meat with a makeshift cleaver on a butcher's block in what passes as her kitchen. Every blow makes the water tremble in her goldfish's bowl. Just as resigned as the humans, it takes everything in stride. From the hallway, the neighbors call to Shuying when they go past her drawn curtain.

"Hey, there, still talking with the *laowai*? You've got a lot to say today," a neighbor comments with a chuckle on her way to the toilet.

I wonder how Shuying will react, but she is on a roll. Unconcerned by the sarcasm, she shrugs her shoulders at the neighbor and smiles.

"We had to leave our children in the village, since we didn't have the papers to stay in Beijing legally. That's not fair, but we couldn't do anything about it. We have no say. We work like animals, and all we hope is that our children will come. Their future is here, in the big cities like Beijing. There is nothing in the village for them: no work, no career, no future, no way to live. We are sacrificing everything for them, and if that doesn't work, they will have to start with nothing, too."

With her *hukou* from Shandong and her parents' limited relations (the famous *guanxi*), the best Shuying's daughter can hope for is a job as a teacher in a village school, or maybe in a regional center. Shuying misses her children very much, but she can't go back home more than four or five times a year because of the cost of traveling. Before she came to Beijing, she couldn't wait to see the capital.

"It's wonderful to see the streets lined with flowers in spring and summer," she admits. "And the city is very clean, but life is too hard here. All we do is work, eat, and sleep. Every time I leave the children, I want to cry. For three days, I can't keep the tears back. My only consolation is how they have gotten used to the separation. Children are a lot more adaptable than adults. All year long, I wait for one thing: summer vacation and New Year. They can come to Beijing and I can enjoy being with them longer. They study all day at the house when we go to work. But in the evening I go shopping with them, and on the weekends we go out into the city. We go to the traditional *hutong* neighborhoods, with narrow alleys and courtyard houses; Tiananmen Square; and the zoo. When it's time for them to leave, the separation is more painful, because I caught a glimpse of the life we could have together. But I have to send them back to the village to be with my parents."

Shuying puts her basin full of kitchen utensils into the big common concrete sink by the entryway to the underground lodgings. She keeps her eyes down as she scrubs away. Her face has turned red and her eyes are wet with tears.

"Oh, no, you're not going to make us break our promise. We'll be afraid to come back and see you."

Brave but heavy with emotion, Shuying laughs, a little embarrassed. It is time for the residents of the underground to do their dishes. Her neighbors glance her way, disapproving. It's better if we leave—but not before we promise to return for another visit.

◆

The aboveground residents of Xibahe Zhongli inhabit another world, completely apart from those below. Like most city dwellers, they have certain prejudices against the *shuzu*. Many of them believe the *mingong* have left work in the fields and come to the city for one reason: to get rich, denying their roots in the process. They also believe that educated people who are not from the cities flock to the big centers just to make money and increase their social status. They refuse to accept, out of prejudice or ignorance, that migrant workers endure enormous hardships and have made essential contributions to urban development.

"They're just common peasants," a second-floor resident complains.

She emerges from her Volkswagen SUV, carrying the elegant clothes that she picked up at the dry cleaners, wrapped in transparent plastic. In her opinion, these louts with manure on their boots make life unlivable for honest city folks like her.

"They come back late and make a lot of noise," she says, shaking her head. "The air stinks down where they live, so they come up and sit in the garden and chatter away under our windows. The men drink beer and throw their cigarette butts on the ground, and burp and spit everywhere. The maintenance costs for the building keep going up because of them. The rats don't pay anything, so they don't give a damn. They're parasites. The government should do something to get rid of them."

Is it harder to feel compassion when you've come a long way, and are only now beginning to enjoy material possessions that weren't available ten or fifteen years ago? The woman is an executive in a private company, and has only one thing in mind: success. To look downward would be like going back to a past she would rather forget.

"Don't they have the right to dream?" we inquire.

"What could they possibly dream about? They have no education, and no future here," she retorts.

"They want to live. They want to provide their children with a better future."

This last remark is deemed unworthy of an answer. The lady executive heads toward her apartment without a goodbye.

◆

I go back to Julong Garden, where the underground residents never bother the ones living on the surface, for one simple reason: the latter don't know they're there. The maintenance staff who serve the people on the upper floors are quiet as mice when they aren't working, and they never loiter on the outdoor paths. The others come out of their holes only to go to their jobs, and they know how to be invisible. Guards make their rounds at night to make sure, among other things, that the staff aren't being a nuisance to the public.

Down below, the dormitory with the fifteen cleaning women shakes off its slumber at around eight p.m. As long as the renters are in their rooms, the door stays open, with only a curtain to mask the hallway light. That way, the women do not wake each other up when they rise and go into the hallway to freshen up over their plastic basins. In front of the entrance to their room, two dusty, staved-in chairs live out the rest of their existence, surrounded by empty bottles and cups of noodles that have attracted a colony of cockroaches. Why bother cleaning up? The garbage is almost a comfort compared to the stinking swamp of the toilets.

The women awake and stretch in their bunk beds, then emerge and turn on the light. Yifei, age thirty-five, came from Gansu province, in the center of China, two years ago. Her short hair is disheveled, she is still in her pajamas, and she yawns uncontrollably, her face worn by fatigue. Every day, she cleans a bar at the Workers' Stadium from eleven in the morning to five in the afternoon, then from nine in the evening to six in the morning. It's the same schedule as her coworkers and roommates. Their boss, who owns a bar and a nightclub where the gilded youth of Beijing come to shake their booties, rents out the Julong Garden dormitory.

"In my village I worked the land," says Yifei, with the proud bearing of someone who has grown up the hard way. "But our plot wasn't any good and didn't produce enough. I came here with my husband. It's easier to find work in Beijing, and the pay is better."

Her husband polishes marble blocks in a factory in the northern suburbs and lives next to his job. Yifei enjoys only four days off a month, so she sees him when his free days coincide with hers, once or twice monthly. The couple is reunited with their seven-year-old daughter, who is being raised by Yifei's in-laws, once a year, for New Year celebrations. They travel loaded down with presents to try to convince the girl to forgive them for leaving her. And to ease their own guilt. Yifei and her husband spend a dozen days with their daughter in Gansu, before returning to their working lives in Beijing.

"That's the hardest thing," she tells me. "It makes me want to cry because we can't watch her grow up. We left her when she was five, and little by little her affection for us has worn away. She hardly wants to talk to us on the phone. We have no authority over her. And my in-laws don't have any, either. The years have exhausted them and they let her do whatever she wants. She's a spoiled child, I'm afraid. And she's not going to change, because we can't do anything about it. If we went back to the village, we wouldn't have the means to raise her, and she wouldn't be any better off."

Wei steps in. "We are missing our children's best years," she says. Now thirty-seven, she came from Shanxi province six years ago. "It's like we're in prison, sentenced to live apart from our children. But we chose this life. It's the only way to give them something better. We'll work ten or fifteen or twenty years in Beijing, to live the best we can and pay for their studies. When we've put a little money aside, we'll go back to our provinces and open a little business. In this dormitory, all of us are married and have children."

Wei has two boys, age eight and eleven. Red-faced and stout, she's not above a little teasing. "Guo is the only one here whose husband doesn't live in Beijing. Don't you think she's pretty? You're not so bad-looking yourself!"

She shakes with laughter, pajamas and all. The women find the whole business hilarious. All except Guo, who is slipping her green plastic basin under her metal bedframe. Her back to us, her figure graceful and slim in her dark gray work uniform and white blouse, she is folding her nightshirt and pulling the sheets from her bed. When she turns in our direction, her pretty face is framed by carefully combed long hair and looks exhausted. She allows herself a little laugh, revealing a disorderly set of teeth, which she hides with her hand.

"I've only been in Beijing three months," she defends herself. "I don't have enough *guanxi* to find a job here for my husband."

Again, the dormitory is flooded with waves of laughter. Guo lowers her head in a display of false modesty, then lifts her walnut-colored eyes in my direction. Suddenly, the heat of the underground lodging is oppressive.

"Admit it, you're better off without him in Beijing," one woman wearing a nightgown says, kneeling on the top bunk, a pillow clasped between her arms and her stomach.

It takes a few more minutes of giggling before the women turn serious again. It is 8:40 and they have to hurry to make it to work on time, but they are still waiting for an answer from this foreigner who has come to offer them a little entertainment.

"I can tell you want to get to work," I say, before leaving myself. "I live just above your dormitory, so I'll come back and be your alarm clock for the evening shift, since you like that so much. But really, I feel sorry for your husbands. If they have to spend a day every month with all of you, they must really suffer."

We share a last laugh. Then the army of women disappears into the great battleground of Beijing.

CHAPTER 6

ABANDONED CHILDREN

Physically, they have nothing in common, yet each time I go through the enormous Beijing West railway station, I think of the one on Friedrichstrasse in Berlin. With its twenty platforms from which the bullet trains depart, along with the more old-fashioned gut-shakers, the endless waiting rooms, the cafés and businesses, Beijing West exemplifies the outsized dimensions of China's monster stations. The one on Friedrichstrasse is on a human scale in comparison. But like Beijing West, the former *Tränenpalast*, or Palace of Tears, the former border crossing between East and West Germany that was located at the Berlin station, was the setting for many heartrending separations. The Westies returned to the free world without knowing when they would see their loved ones again, stuck back in the East.

One day, as we were waiting at Beijing West, I told a local friend that after reunification, Germany opened the surveillance files compiled by the Stasi (the East German state security service) so that everyone could discover who among their close friends and family had spied and informed on them. My friend was incredulous.

"We'll never see that in China," she insisted. "The regime is nowhere near giving up. There are 1.3 billion of us, overseen by an obsessive bureaucracy. Can you imagine the miles of archives people would have to dig through? If we ever change our political system one day, we'll just have to turn our backs on the past without demanding that justice be done. Otherwise, we'd lapse into chaos, and no one wants that kind of disorder in China. With such a big population it would be a catastrophe, completely out of control."

Waiting for the day when things would open up, my friend ran out of patience. She immigrated to Canada a year after I came to Beijing.

Her words return to me every time I go through the Beijing West station. With their rough packs on their backs, their improvised picnics, their buying frenzy when they see the many products —from the most useful to the most frivolous—that are available in a big urban center like Beijing, the passengers returning to the provinces remind me of other travelers I have seen. I can't help thinking of the East Germans who came to West Berlin to discover the great department stores like KaDeWe. The relative poverty of the province dwellers and their rough country clothes stand out among Beijing's prosperity. The two worlds cohabit in China as well: the privileged city folk and the country mice.

◆

On this Sunday evening at Beijing West station, parents are accompanying their daughter, who is returning to her boarding school in Hengshui, in the southern reaches of Hebei province, some 270 kilometers (170 miles) away. In Western countries, it is often the well-off students who study at prestigious private schools. In Beijing, it's the other way around. Separated from their parents, the children of *mingong* head for boarding schools in their home province, since their *hukou* won't allow them to register at a public school in the big city. While middle-class parents are spending fortunes on tutors and private lessons, to bump up their children's grades and provide them with the best possible future, the *mingong* are fighting for their children's right to go to school at all. The rat people are making tremendous sacrifices. It's a matter, sometimes, of life and death.

Wearing her school uniform—a blue and white suit—Pei Xiaotong, ten years old, waves goodbye to her parents with a grim smile, after her five days with them in Beijing. Ninety percent of the students at her school are the children of *mingong*. The schedules have been arranged so that those whose parents can afford to buy a ticket can join them several times a year in Beijing for five-day periods. Xiaotong has been making the trip to see her parents for five years now, though they have never gotten used to the long separations, and they have trouble holding back their tears. Her parents sell vegetables at the market, working from five a.m. to ten p.m., every day. Even when Xiaotong comes to visit, they hardly have any time to be with her.

"Technically, we can sign our children up for school in Beijing," says her father, Pei Yong, watching the train pull away. Big and well built, with the hands of a boxer, his jeans pulled up above his hips and held in place with a belt, slouching in his black vinyl jacket, he has the physique of a man who wouldn't let anything stand in his way. But he has to bend to the system's rules.

"But in reality, public school is not for us. They want seven different documents, including one that says we own an apartment here and have an employment contract. Of course that's impossible for us. With what I make, there's no way I could buy an apartment in this city. At first, my daughter didn't want to leave. She thought we were trying to abandon her. Finally, I convinced her that her school could open doors to a university here and give her some kind of future."

The law requires everyone to receive nine years of free schooling, so over the last several years the bigger cities have allowed migrants to send their children to school, even without a *hukou*, but they demand a plethora of administrative documents. In 2014, Beijing launched the five document system, wherein parents had to submit five different papers, such as proof of residence and employment. This was designed to keep thirty percent of migrant children out of the school system. Some districts set up supplementary demands: both parents had to reside and work in the neighborhood around the school, which excluded migrants who make long trips from one urban center to the next for their work. Some authorities require proof of payment of health insurance and ownership of property. Other parents, when they do show up with the papers, are told that their child will not be accepted anyway. According to the liberal newspaper *Southern Weekly*, restrictions aimed at migrants to the capital keep tens of thousands of Chinese children out of school. Official statistics, which tend to minimize the phenomenon, estimate the number of children excluded from public education in Beijing to be 140,000.

The party is aware of the problem and has declared its determination to extend greater rights to its bottom dogs. But at the same time, in 2015, China decided to strictly limit the population size of big urban centers and direct migrants toward midsize cities, for which authorities promised to grant 100 million resident permits by 2020. Local party authorities decided to level off the capital's population by limiting it to 23 million in the same year, but many experts don't think Beijing's population needs to be restricted. The real problem is that China has underinvested in education. Today, Beijing has only 1,000 elementary schools, compared to 1,800 in 2000, while the population has jumped by sixty percent. Of course, a number of private institutions have sprung up to fill the gap, but since they are not part of the official education system, many of them are not accredited to send their students to university entrance exams. And those private schools that do have accreditation have the same admission standards as public schools.

According to figures put forward by the Communist Youth League's newspaper, *Beijing Youth Daily*, several thousand children living in Beijing, the offspring of *mingong*, are going to boarding schools in Hebei. But despite the solitude and their problems adapting, they are actually the lucky ones. Most *mingong* living in the Beijing underground can't afford to send their children to these schools. The vast majority leave them behind in their home villages. The All-China Women's Federation (ACWF) estimates that more than 61 million abandoned children were living in the countryside, looked after by grandparents or other close family members, in 2013. Another group, some 5 percent, according to ACWF estimates, are completely on their own and live on money sent by their parents. The *liushou ertong* have come to represent some 37.7 percent of the young rural population and 22 percent of all children in the country. Caught in the greatest wave of migration in human history, their parents headed for the big cities in search of work. Duan Chengrong, a professor of demography at Renmin University in Beijing who participated in the ACWF study, believes that in 2019 the number of abandoned children stands between 65 million and 66 million, whereas the number of *mingong* has reached some 270 million. He bases his projections on the last national census in 2010.

◆

When classes are over for the day, only a few grandparents make the trip to the Tangxi public school. In this distant village in Jiangxi province, one of the poorest in the People's Republic, most students are *liushou ertong*, or left-behind children, now that their parents have gone looking for work in the country's big cities. Like the millions of children left behind across rural China, the students of this small outpost impatiently count the days until New Year, when, finally, after months of separation, they will be reunited with their parents.

Squatting on the ground of an alleyway lined with run-down houses made of brick and gray tile, dressed in rags, his face streaked with dirt, nine-year-old Xiaohai watches a friend play on his phone as he chews on grilled chicken feet in a plastic bag. He's on his way home from school on his own and stopped to play.

"My grandparents work in the fields," he says, pointing to a distant hut, a spot of gray in the midst of the rice paddies, brown in the winter and crisscrossed with muddy footpaths.

When it comes to homework, his illiterate grandparents aren't much help.

"I get along on my own. That's the way it is," he murmurs, his eyes glued to the phone screen, scratching away at his runny nose with black fingernails.

Exhausted by years of labor, his substitute mother and father, both nearly seventy years old, provide the bare minimum for Xiaohai: a roof, a bed, meals, and a little affection. For the rest, he is on his own while they work. His parents look after his material needs. Every month, they send the small amounts of money they are able to put aside. He sees them once a year at most, sometimes once every other year.

"They promised they would come to the village for this New Year." The celebration follows the lunar calendar and usually takes place in February. "Last year, they couldn't find train tickets."

Hardened by the long separations, Xiaohai claims to be totally indifferent to whether they come or not. "It means nothing," he says, but soon he admits, with tears in his eyes, that he misses his parents and often thinks of them.

He can't remember what city they live in or how they are earning a living. The boy knows only that they are working in a factory, too far away to return more than once a year.

"I write them letters with the school," he tells us. "But they don't always write back. Sometimes they call, but not too often. This year, they forgot my birthday."

His parents never ask how he is doing at school, and they have no contact with the teachers.

The *liushou ertong* have been sacrificed on the altar of Chinese economic growth, which has increased at a phenomenal rate. All along the road that passes through a series of small villages, from Tangxi to Yichun—the closest town, seventy kilometers (forty-five miles) away—children play with stones in the dirt. Some of them, when they get too exhausted, sleep by the side of the road, with big trucks rolling at top speed right past their heads. Separated from their parents at birth, the *liushou ertong* wander through childhood and adolescence with no one to look after their health, be it physical, emotional, or psychological.

"These children have no structure or schedule," explains Yi Zhibing, the former director of a kindergarten for abandoned children in Yichun, who has gone back to being a teacher in one of the villages. "They run along the roads and play there until they drop from exhaustion. Some are hit by cars. Others drown in the ponds."

He may look like a cop, solidly built beneath his washed-out jeans and thick leather jacket, but Yi Zhibing is afraid of what the neighbors might say about him—to be seen with a foreigner is risky business. He leads us away from his house, to a deserted road, to describe the daily life of these children, chain-smoking all the while. Soon, our car is filled with a thick gray cloud. The smoke and the sheer brutality of his stories has my head spinning, and I can barely keep up.

The media report regularly on these tragedies. In 2015, the deaths of four children, abandoned by migrant parents, had all of China in lamentations. The letter found by the body of the oldest child indicated it was suicide: they had died after swallowing pesticides.

"Thank you for your kindness. I know you wanted to do good for us, but it is time to leave now," the letter said. "I vowed I would not live past fifteen," the oldest wrote. "I am now fourteen. I dream of death, but the dream never comes true. Today, it must finally become reality."

The bodies of the four children, a boy and three girls between five and fourteen years old, were discovered in a house in a small village in the Bijie region, in Guizhou province, that is known for its poverty. According to the investigation, they had lived there alone since 2014. Their father left the village to look for work and sent back 700 yuan (US$100) a month to look after the family. Their mother left as well, to Guangdong province, the country's industrial heartland, after a fight with the father, which she had reported as domestic violence. Since then, the children had been feeding themselves from a corn crop that their father had planted, and they had left school long ago.

The mother of the four Bijie victims, Ren Xifen, thirty-two years old, returned from Guangdong, where she was working in a toy factory, to attend the funeral.

"I didn't look after my responsibilities," she admitted, after viewing the bodies of her children before cremation. She explained that after the fight with her husband, she didn't "have the strength to go back home. I really did abandon them." Ren said regretfully, "I'm illiterate. I can't even write my name. I wanted them to do good at school, not like I did, so their lives wouldn't be so hard. All I want to do now is go where they went."

Many parent associations blame the government for not organizing a system of boarding schools to take care of *mingong* children abandoned in the villages, while their parents live like rats in the country's gleaming metropolises.

A veritable wave of criticism poured down via social media after the suicides. Despite the censors employed to erase sensitive information that appears online, the Communist Party is unable to dampen the anger when such deaths occur.

"Abandoned children are the ones sacrificed to runaway urbanization. The state invests too much in big public schools that serve only the privileged, and not enough in the rural areas. This is extreme exploitation and injustice for the peasants," wrote Feng Dou Zhong on the Weibo social media site.

"The *hukou* system created this tragedy. What parents don't love their children? Who wants to be separated from their children and have to go work elsewhere?" wondered Yuan Yuan Er, also on Weibo.

The premier of the State Council, Li Keqiang, ordered an inquiry, judging that the People's Republic could not "let such a tragedy happen again."

But this was just the most recent in a series of tragedies that had befallen abandoned children. In 2013, the case of five boys, cousins aged nine to thirteen, who died in a dumpster in Guizhou province, the southwestern part of the country, disgusted the nation and attracted attention to the sad fate of the *liushou ertong*. Their parents had left in search of work in the coastal regions, the industrial heart of the country where the thirst for laborers seems to be insatiable. Without an adult to look after them during their short lives, they became street children. In the heart of winter, in search of shelter, they climbed into the large wheeled container and lit a fire to keep warm. The children died from carbon monoxide poisoning.

In 2009, a boy and a girl drowned in a nearby village after falling into a well. Another boy, in the care of his grandfather, died after eating rat poison. Consumed by guilt, the man committed suicide shortly after. The parent associations point out that many abandoned children die in such circumstances every year, but since there are no official statistics about the number of deaths, the public hears only about the most striking cases picked up by the media and social networks.

The psychological impact on children separated from their parents is rarely discussed. Fifteen percent of left-behind children suffer from mental disorders, and nearly fifty percent are affected by psychological problems, notably depression and anxiety, as well behavioral issues resulting from feelings of inferiority and lack of self-confidence. According to statistics from the Chinese Ministry of Justice, seventy percent of juvenile delinquents are left-behind children. Rural areas are populated by at least 20 million children who have dropped out of school and have no training—one young villager in ten. And nearly seventy percent of left-behind children are unable to understand what is being discussed in the classroom, according to government figures. Many of them turn to alcohol and drugs, whereas others become gamers and spend all their time in cybercafés. A boy of fifteen living on his own broke into an apartment and killed the owner for 300 yuan (US$40). He told police he needed money to pay for his internet connection. Meanwhile, his father was working low-paying odd jobs in Guangzhou.

The little village of Tangxi will be forever marked by the tragedy of May 6, 2012. That day, five children from the Wang family—Yubo, age six; Yizu and Xinman, ten; and Baoting and Baolan, eleven—drowned. They had jumped into a pond to escape the stifling heat, but they did not know how to swim.

Years later, the memory of that tragic day remains painful for Wang Jiushou and his wife, Li Xixiu, in their mid-seventies, who were looking after their eight grandchildren. In front of the door of their modest house, her frail body perched on a bamboo stool, Li Xixiu wipes her tears on the back of her sleeve. Her husband, chain-smoking cigarettes rolled from yellowish paper, puffs away and sobs. Wearing a blue cap as old as the earth and a threadbare jacket, he stares into space from a face like old parchment, saying the same words over and over again: "I still can't believe I lost my grandchildren that way."

The woman next door makes a gesture with her hand—the grandfather has lost his mind. Duoyou and I are a little ashamed at having come and stirred up bad memories. Suddenly, we just want to get back in the car and leave the grandparents alone with their pain.

But Li Xixiu cares nothing for our scruples. In a sea of uninterrupted words, she makes her confession, as if trying to exorcise her sorrow. Lucid but tormented by guilt, she doesn't seem to notice her husband's state. The day of the tragedy, she was the first to hear the children calling for help. Immediately, she had a bad feeling and rushed to the pond. She didn't know how to swim either. She called her husband to get help in the village. Wang begged the neighbors to come and lend a hand, but without success.

"All the young people have left the village. When something like that happens, there's no one around to help," he murmurs. "You are alone, alone, alone ..."

With no other choice, Li called a taxi as the children screamed for help in the brackish water. She went to the next village for help, and when she returned with two young men, it was too late to save her grandchildren. Recounting the story has left her emotionally and physically exhausted. She takes her small round face in her hands, and her tears flow. Finally, she catches her breath and tells us, "We work hard, and we see to the meals and take the children to school, but we can't keep an eye on them all the time. It is too much for us. We are just too old to raise children."

She agrees that her two sons had no other option than to leave their children in her care and go look for work in the coastal regions. They went to Shenzhen, the great metropolis in the south, ground zero of the economic opening launched by Deng Xiaoping at the end of the 1970s, located across from Hong Kong, nearly 800 kilometers (500 miles) south of their village.

"My sons did what all the young people in the village have done. They went to make a living so their children wouldn't starve to death. Here, besides growing rice and potatoes, or making canola oil, there's nothing. The companies don't come here, to these mountains, far from everything," she says, shaking her head.

As if it were a misfortune, Li Xixiu explains that her sons had only girls at first, but they continued having children until they finally got boys because, "according to tradition, you have to have boys"—even though they knew they didn't have the means to take care of them. Then the bureaucratic steamroller started moving with the implacable harshness it is known for. Her sons had violated the one-child policy, and more than once. They were fined an astronomical amount, the equivalent of ten years' salary.

"Before the tragedy, the bureaucrats harassed us almost every day, trying to make us pay," Li Xixiu says angrily. "One day they showed up with workers who started smashing the house with sledgehammers. They warned us they would tear the place down, but we couldn't pay them what we didn't have. Because we have nothing. The fine was simply impossible to pay."

Since the tragedy that attracted national and international media attention, the authorities have left the family in peace, but the fine has not been officially suspended, or canceled. The bureaucrats could come storming back at any time, based on a local enforcement order. Despite President Xi Jinping's promise to reform the country so it will be governed "according to law," arbitrary decisions are made at every level. After the children's deaths, Wang Guangjun, the younger son who lost his two little girls, moved to Yichun with his wife, where he and his brother found work in construction. The couple took back their surviving child.

"Luckily, we still have a son left. We will never go and work in some other city, no matter how hard things are. Now, the most important thing is to be with him," the man swears, still living with the regret.

Li Xixiu adds, "Children are always better off with their parents. They won't listen to us. They'd rather go and play with their friends than do their homework. Their parents can discipline them and pay attention to their schoolwork."

Chased by a rooster flapping its wings, a flock of chickens pecks at crumbs on the floor of the main room, a rough concrete slab. The dining room table is surrounded by at least a dozen chairs, but big family meals are a thing of the past.

"Stay and have lunch with us. The house is so empty," Li Xixiu offers.

She throws some vegetables and pieces of chicken into a wok, adding chilies and other spices, and mixing everything together with chopsticks. The rice, prepared in an electric pot from another century, is ready. But my stomach contracts. I am not hungry, and neither is Duoyou. We make an attempt at the food as politely as possible, as the grandmother and her husband devour the contents of their plates. Their appetite is frightening to see. I am overwhelmed by their hunger that has pursued them for decades. Eating, surviving, has become an obsession for them, wiping away anything else. I note down one last sentence, then decide it is time for us to be on our way.

"Our sons aren't angry with us, but we don't see them very often anymore," Li Xixiu says sadly. "The grandchildren call us a few times a week to say they miss us."

At the Tangxi school, the district principal points out that seventy percent of the children in the system live without their parents.

"The biggest problem is the lack of love," he says. "We try to make up for it by sending the teachers to visit the students at home regularly, with some small gifts. We help them write to their parents. And we try and stay in contact with the parents to let them know how their children are doing."

Tipped off by the school, the secretary of the district Communist Party joins the conversation. The subject of children who have died is deemed "sensitive" by the local authorities. Duoyou and I sense that our incognito visit to the village is over. Normally, party officials arrive with an escort of police who demand that we show permission from the central government or local authorities, a clear impossibility. Chinese administration has an unequaled talent when it comes to burying journalists' requests concerning sensitive subjects. After checking passports and papers, the police normally choose between two options: taking us to the nearest airport, or accompanying us in a manner so ostentatious that no one will dare say a word to us, or even look our way. But this time we get lucky: the party secretary came on his own. After asking for the usual mountain of authorizations that we don't have, he agrees to talk.

"Since the tragedy happened, everyone has realized that children are the future of the family and the country," the local official states, once we have promised we will protect his identity.

He takes off his glasses, sighs, slides them into the pocket of his white shirt, and then stands up, slapping the hem of his pants to get the dust off. I keep my notebook under wraps so that he will trust us, but he seems to have cut the conversation short, and Duoyou and I are afraid he will end up sabotaging what remains of our stay in the region. We wait and watch, and then suddenly, he sits down again.

"Luckily, everything has become simpler thanks to today's means of communication," he goes on, as if he never hesitated. "We have a major program to create jobs by attracting business to the Yichun region. Families that are able to make a salary of 4,000 yuan [US$570] a month in the big urban centers farther away now prefer to move closer and live in midsized cities. The families are happy with a salary of 3,000 yuan [US$425] so that they can see their children more often, or live with them."

After thinking hard, the party official cannot name a single company intending to move to Yichun.

"It's not easy attracting business and creating employment here," he concedes. "In the village, all the people of working age have left. Only children and old folks are left."

Yi Zhibing, the former director of the *liushou ertong* kindergarten, throws up his arms in despair, dispersing a thick cloud of smoke.

"He's all talk! They don't do anything for the kids," he says angrily. "All the public schools are concerned with is the quality of the teaching. But the reality is this: left-behind children are on their own. In the thirty years I've been doing this job, I never got a single call from one of their parents, even when a kid was sick. The grandparents feed them, but that's all. When they hit adolescence, the kids go to the cybercafé and fall under all sorts of bad influences. Their parents send enough money to see to their needs, but the boys waste it. They steal and find all kinds of schemes to make more money. The girls fall in love too soon and ruin their lives. We have a false value in this society: parents are supposed to sacrifice their children for the sake of money. Where is the profit if the kids are kept out of school, if they're unhappy or grow up to be good-for-nothings and delinquents?"

In the People's Republic, fifty percent of the population lives in the cities, and that figure will rise to seventy percent in the coming decades. Jobs are not about to return to the countryside.

The feeling of abandonment pushes some children to run away, taking the train illegally to the city in hopes of finding their parents. For left-behind children, seeing their parents is a luxury. The cases of kids between seven and fourteen who have been caught and sent home by the police are countless. Suicide is frequent among these young runaways.

◆

In January 2014, Xiao Lin went to school to pick up his report card by himself. Most of his classmates were accompanied by their parents. Lin was nine years old. His mother and father had divorced and left the village of Sige, in Anhui province, shortly after he was born. That day, he seemed disappointed by his grades. His mother called that evening to tell him she wouldn't be coming for New Year, a few weeks later. Over dinner, he was quiet. No one under his roof suspected he would take his life a few hours later by hanging himself with a rope in the bathroom. He left no word.

Lin was exactly thirty days old when his father left him. It was his mother's turn a few months later. His parents never came to pick up a single report card, according to Yang Qinglin, the school principal. They never attended a single parent-teacher meeting and rarely phoned him, which contributed to the boy's feeling of insecurity.

"Lin had more discipline than other students, because he knew he would have no one to defend him if he ever caused trouble at school," Yang remembers.

After Lin's suicide, his father wasn't sure about going to the funeral. He didn't want to leave his job for fear of losing it.

◆

At the end of December 2013, another event gained traction online. It started with a strange little note stuck on the locked door of the Jianba, a barbershop in Zhuzhou in southern China. The note surprised the regular customers:

"Dear friends, I received a phone call from my daughter yesterday. I have been away from her too long. She has forgotten how to call me Daddy. I beg you for one week's break to spend with my family."

A passerby took a picture of the message and posted it on Weibo.

Wu Hongwei, the barber who had taped the note to the door, and his wife, Wang Yuan, had left their daughter with her grandparents in a distant village 540 kilometers (335 miles) from

Zhuzhou, when she was nine months old. Numerous Chinese media outlets told their story. The couple described how they suffered from having missed their daughter's first words and first steps, never thinking they would be away so long. At first, everything went well for them, and their new life in the city seemed full of promise. Wu had left his village of Zhaishi in the Hunan mountains at age twenty-four. Had he stayed, he would have worked for the miserable salary of 15 yuan (US$2.15) a day. He climbed on a bus with his uncle and headed for Zhangzhou, where he found a spot as an apprentice barber, for no remuneration at all.

A few years later, he settled in Zhuzhou, where he charmed Wang with folk songs he played on his guitar. Their daughter, Beibei, was born in 2011, and Wang left her job selling cell phones to take care of the baby. Meanwhile, Wu worked like the devil, from morning until eleven at night, to try to compensate for the loss of a second salary. Then came a cruel blow when the pediatrician informed them that their daughter absolutely needed powdered baby formula. This was around the time of the 2008 scandal of milk poisoned with melamine that sickened 300,000 babies across China and killed 6. Everyone was afraid of buying contaminated formula. The couple spent a fifth of their monthly salary of 3,000 yuan (US$425), on quality formula for their child. That was the end of their plan for Wu to leave his job and join his wife and daughter in the village, and Wang was forced to go back to work in the city.

The couple did everything in their power to maintain their connection to their daughter. As often as they could, they made the fourteen-hour trip by train, bus, and motorcycle to spend time with her. Wu had only one goal in mind: to cut as many people's hair at 15 yuan (US$2.15) a head to pay for the travel and send money to his parents. The couple called their daughter every day to tell her how much they loved her. They taped photos of themselves on the concrete walls of her bedroom in her grandparents' house. Wang cried at night when she smelled her daughter's pajamas; they had gotten too small and she had brought them back with her.

"We told ourselves that at least she wouldn't have to face the pressures of living in the city, and that we had turned to the same solution most adults use when they have to leave home and work elsewhere," Wang remembers.

Then there was one visit to the village that turned into an ordeal. When they tried to hold Beibei, she ran away, calling for her grandmother. When the couple asked her who her mother and father were, she disappeared into her room and pointed to the photos on the wall, not making the connection between them and the two adults standing in front of her. She had been raised speaking the village dialect and couldn't understand her mother. The couple showered gifts on the girl, but when evening came, she wanted to sleep in her grandmother's arms. The couple replaced the older woman only once their daughter was fast asleep.

"Those few hours were precious," Wu says. "But for Beibei, 'Daddy' and 'Mommy' didn't mean anything anymore. They were sounds that had no emotion behind them."

"I wanted so much to teach her what it means to be a mother," Wang adds. "I wanted her to understand that the mother gives birth to the child and shows her how to talk, walk, and sing. A mother watches her child grow up. She is the human being closest to her."

After those events, Wang and Wu wanted their daughter to come and live with them in the city permanently, but their underground rathole, urban pollution, the pressure-filled life, and low-quality food convinced them she would be better off in the country. They send for her as often as possible, to share moments of their city life, but they decided to wait for her to grow up a little more, and for their economic situation to improve, so that they could offer her a decent place to live where she could stay full time.

"It's complicated," Wang admits. "But I haven't given up on teaching her the real meaning of the word 'mother' one day."

◆

Lost in the midst of a forest of giant bamboo, surrounded by fields of cotton and corn on one side, and terraced green hills of orchards on the other, stands the little village of Huaixi, Tangxi's neighbor. Eighty percent of the inhabitants of this bucolic hamlet, the kind where you might expect to see Heidi wandering by, are children living without their parents. We spent two whole days here without seeing a single adult. At first glance, the place seems to offer nothing to the passing traveler. A flock of grandmothers, sitting on brightly colored, low plastic chairs in front of the grocery, sip tea and gossip. Each time we came by, they fell silent, the better to observe us. Visitors are rare in Huaixi. A foreigner with white skin is an absolute curiosity.

"This is the first time we've ever seen a *laowai* around here," one of the women announces proudly. She is wearing the village uniform: gray pants and a worn blue shirt. "Where do you come from?"

The atmosphere is a little heavy, and I try to make a joke. Maybe I will manage to lighten up the proceedings.

"I come from Africa," I tell them.

Not a good idea. The women look at one another in disbelief.

"Try and guess," I say.

"Don't you think he looks like an American?" one of them asks, squinting at me through little round glasses perched on her nose.

"Not at all. He's too little," another declares, her flowered dress not quite matching her pink imitation Crocs.

"He could be German," a third guesses, scratching her hair dyed jet-black, the favorite color of Chinese women of all social classes.

"Not big enough," the second one repeats.

"I saw a documentary about Norway on CCTV, and I can guarantee that he looks like a Norwegian," a fourth woman declares.

For the good ladies, I am Norwegian, though none of them has ever heard of the place, other than the discerning TV-watcher with a taste for public television. I can't convince them that I'm French. *Faguoren* is a joke to them; I'm either too blond or too big or not romantic enough. They are just as doubtful about my supposed credentials as a sociologist. Sharper when it comes to what foreigners do for a living, they immediately sniff out the journalist in me.

"Ah, you've come for the *liushou ertong*!" the first grand-mother exclaims. "Well, you're in luck. We're waiting for the bell to take the kids for lunch."

I start to relax a little; the ice has been broken. One of those Chinese miracles has just occurred, and the old woman is ready to talk. When people who have been around the block in China decide to open up, they can say just about anything.

"All of us are raising our grandchildren," she adds. "It's no fun. I'm seventy years old and I work in the fields all day. The only break is when I wait for the two boys at noon. When I come home exhausted after my day, the kids make me run a race. I'm not young enough to fight with them to do their lessons. I tell them they'll end up at the factory like their parents. They couldn't care less. Their grandfather has even less patience than me."

The bell sounds and the women get up stiffly.

"It's been like this since the 1980s," says Ren Jiqing, a fifty-seven-year-old grandfather, sitting on his electric scooter in front of the school entrance, waiting for his granddaughter to show up. "It's normal to be an abandoned child. Of course the kids complain about growing up without their parents, but if they don't know how to swallow bitterness, they'll never get anywhere in life."

His granddaughter, Mei Lun, age eleven, comes out, wearing her classic school uniform: a white-and-blue blazer. Playing with her long ponytail, she doesn't agree with Ren Jiqing.

"Only rich kids live with their parents. They're lucky—their parents don't have to go far away to work and they see them all the time. They're easy to spot. They have the best clothes," she adds in a quiet voice, admitting she cries several times a week when she thinks of her parents.

"Her parents send us 4,000 or 5,000 yuan [US$570–715] a year to cover school tuition, and buy food and clothes," Ren Jiqing explains. "In the city, the cost of living is much higher: rent, food, tuition, clothes. They couldn't live with their children. They don't have a choice. Anyway, going to school in a city would do nothing for Mei Lun. She's not much of a student. More like horse horse tiger tiger."

The Chinese expression means so-so. A craftsman who makes objects and furniture out of bamboo, Ren Jiqing is as straightforward in his judgment as Chinese people can be. Adept at manipulating the art of circumlocution and dissimulation to keep from offending someone because of their opinions about daily life, they can still be harsh when they want to be. However, Mei Lun, who wears a hangdog look, is third in her class, an honorable position.

"Her grades are all right for a little school in a nowhere village in our province," he declares. "But imagine where she'd place in a better school. She'd be lost."

Ren Jiqing admits he didn't hang around in a classroom very long, and he can't help her with her homework. Like most of her classmates, Mei Lun gets along on her own.

A dozen students in white blazers and running shoes gather around us by the exit, while younger kids slip past, then break out giggling as they run away. Their favorite game is comparing their feet to mine. They might as well have come face-to-face with a unicorn, they are that intrigued and surprised. A little boy ventures a question: "Do all *laowai* have feet this big? How do you walk?" Uproarious laughter greets his comment.

Among the fifteen students I count, only one girl is being raised by one of her parents. Fang, a girl of thirteen, tells me she lives with her grandparents, who are more than seventy. They haven't come to the school for pickup. She is holding her little sister by the hand so that she can't escape.

"I take care of her," she says, pulling at her short haircut. "My grandparents can't. They're too old."

Her parents have gone to work farther south, in the province of Fujian. She knows nothing of what they do or how they live. She talks to them on the phone four or five times a month. But their short conversations touch on only routine subjects such as her lessons, her grades, and admonitions to help out her grandparents. Every morning, Fang gets up at six and makes breakfast: a bowl of soup with noodles and vegetables. At noon, her grandmother has lunch ready when she comes back with her little sister. In the evening, after school, she runs errands, and then prepares the vegetables for dinner. After, she cleans up and keeps an eye on her sister's homework. Only then can Fang do her own lessons. She assumes these responsibilities, a crushing burden for a child her age, without complaint. Though she bursts into tears once she turns off the light in the evening, in bed, claiming she doesn't know why.

"I see my parents once a year," she says. "For New Year, the best time of all. A month ahead of time, I'm so happy I can't sleep. I miss my father the most. We're very close. He's the best father in the world."

CHAPTER 7

YOUTH DENIED

A plastic statuette in garish colors, mass produced by the millions in one of those countless factories in the southern reaches of the world's workshop, in the typical kitschy style of the new Chinese Empire, occupies pride of place at the entrance to the labyrinth. We are in the first level of the basement of the Yangqiao Xili Building, located at the edge of the 3rd Ring Road in the center of Beijing. A variety of offerings, dried mandarins and used sticks of incense, honor Cai Shen, the god of wealth. Both Buddhism and Taoism acknowledge that he has the power to improve a person's financial situation. Some less devout individuals have thrown their cigarette butts in his direction. The atmosphere of this rathole is definitely college dorm. Skateboards, scooters, and Rollerblades lie in heaps by the doors to the forty or so rooms. The hallway ceilings are crisscrossed by wires for hanging out laundry: brightly colored underwear, red, yellow, and green, some displaying Hello Kitty, still the idol of young Asians, along with T-shirts with the insignia of the local soccer team: the Beijing Sinobo Guoan.

We knock at a makeshift door, which disintegrates under our hands.

"*You ren ma?*" Duoyou asks—"Anyone home?"

After a few tries, a young woman with short hair sticking up in all directions, eyes heavy with fatigue, wearing Maisy Mouse pajamas, opens up. It is five in the afternoon, and Zhao Mengying was sleeping like a log. A friend, with long, well-coiffed hair and an ecru dress with lace flounces, is lying next to her. She came in from the country the day before to visit Mengying and was very much awake but didn't dare open the door. The two young women are from the little village of Anyu, in the distant province of Henan, and they blush when we announce why we're here. After some hesitation, they finally allow us to enter their six-square-meter (sixty-five-square-foot) room.

Unembarrassed, eighteen-year-old Mengying lies down under the pink blanket on her double bed that takes up half the room and tells us to sit on the mattress. Her village friend doesn't know what to make of this arrangement. She hasn't moved or made the slightest sound. Two damp towels hang from a rusty nail on the back wall next to a small cracked mirror. Leftover rice and chicken steep in an oily wok. Mengying's message is loud and clear: in Beijing, she has found the life she always wanted.

She is a waitress in a hotel in the Beijing Nan Zhan, the Beijing South railway station. At fifteen, she left her village and the inhospitable nest her peasant parents provided for her. Her mother spent her entire life in Anyu, raising her two children. Her father, however, lived the life of a *mingong* for fifteen years, moving from construction sites to the factories in the big coastal cities, the leading edge of the country's growth. In the end, he returned to the land when his eldest son left home to work in Jiangsu province, where he helps build houses. One less mouth to feed meant the father could return to the village with his handful of savings, which were not even enough to open the grocery store he'd dreamed of.

At first, Mengying found a job at a hairdresser's in one of the innumerable, soulless Chinese cities, 100 kilometers (60 miles) from her village. Despite her inexperience, she soon understood it was a bad deal. The distance was too great for her to return home in the evening and the salary too meager for her to live like a human being. So she was swept up in the great *mingong* migration. Her first step was to Handan, a "midsize" seat of local government of almost 10 million inhabitants in Hebei province, that surrounds the capital. Her job was selling appliances in a big department store. Finally, she made the move to Beijing in January 2014.

For five months Mengying has lived in her little underground room, a five-minute walk from her work. She found the place in a special section of the rooms for rent ads and pays 700 yuan (US$100) a month, cold water and electricity included. At that price, a person can't expect much in the way of luxury. The tiles that started out white show stains of uncertain origin. Electrical wires run this way and that. She hangs metal hangers on them to dry her clothes. Hot water sets her back another 60 yuan (US$8.50) a month, and access to Wi-Fi costs the same but is an indispensable link to the outside world, since no cell phone signal can penetrate these underground chambers.

"At the hotel, I work twenty-four hours at a stretch, from nine in the morning to nine the next morning, one day out of two," she tells us. "When I'm at home, all I do is sleep. This is the perfect place to do it. There's no window—it's practically a tomb. At first, I had trouble breathing normally because the air is so bad, but I got used to it. And it's not so cold in winter. I don't see why I'd spend more to live somewhere else. The only problem is the owner—he's not very tolerant. I always have to pay the rent exactly on time. And I always end up getting cheated. The other day a friend from the hotel visited. He was a little drunk and he knocked down the door. I had to pay a 100-yuan [15 dollars] penalty and the door still isn't fixed."

Her former classmate looks at the door with some amusement. It's taped together with pieces of cardboard fitted more or less in place. She found a job as a teacher in the village school; big-city life has no appeal for her.

"I'd rather stay in the village, even if it's less thrilling. Living like a rat means living without light," she declares, then rubs her hands together nervously.

The two friends burst out giggling.

"At least it's good for the skin here," Mengying says a minute later. "There's no danger of getting a tan. My skin stays nice and pale. Plenty of girls who live on the surface envy me."

Two evenings a week, on Friday or Saturday and one weekday, Mengying works in a karaoke bar as a "companion." When groups of young men show up for their evening festivities, they rent private rooms equipped with a giant screen. They order beer by the case and choose girls they want to warble away with in front of a microphone, then pass the baton to the next guy, dropping onto the sofa with a cigarette. Every guy is accompanied by the young woman he has chosen for "romantic duets." Mengying's two jobs together bring in 4,000 yuan (US$570) a month. Once she has paid her rent, bills, and food, there is not much left for luxuries, like clothes.

"Some of the boys are fine," she goes on, sitting cross-legged on her bed. "But others think they can feel us up and touch our hair. But we're not paid for that. The karaoke where I work is a proper place and doesn't offer sexual services. When they're boys my age, sometimes I go along with them, but the old men are repulsive. They're always most aggressive when they've had something to drink. They insult the owner like she's a *mamasan*" —a madam—"and we're her whores."

Saunas, karaoke bars, and certain hairdressing salons are reputed to be places of prostitution. Officially, the "happy ending" is not on offer, but something extra can often be negotiated with young women employees for a handful of yuan, since they make hardly enough to live on. The owner will look the other way— as long as he gets his cut. Mengying hopes for a better future and surrenders to her wildest dreams as she drops into sleep, completely exhausted.

"It's a little silly," she realizes, blushing and lowering her eyes, as if caught out in a contradiction, "but ever since I read online about that worker who became one of the richest women in China, with her billions of dollars, I've been thinking I could start my own business, too. Why not? With a little luck, I could be the richest woman in China."

Mengying and her friend dissolve into giggles again. By revealing her most intimate private thoughts, she has lost face by divulging too much. Only a quick reversal will allow her to recover. She launches into a fantasy tirade: "President Xi is going to help me. He's going to open an eight-star hotel for me and I'll make a fortune. All the men will throw themselves at my feet and I'll marry the most handsome one. Then I'll go back to the village and live like a queen."

Fairy tales are rare in China. The Red princes of the Communist Party don't pay attention to rats. How many millions of people are languishing at the bottom of the ladder despite their yearning to succeed? Who can tell? I ask Mengying what the chances are that her most realistic dream will come true anytime soon.

"It's ninety-nine to one that it won't come true. Actually, the only thing I can hope for is to marry a good guy and have a life that's not too terrible and a job a little less nasty after a few years, but it won't be much better paid."

Intrigued by the noise and the conversation in a foreign language, the girl in the next room comes into the hallway in her yellow, fake silk pajamas. Tall and elegant, her pretty face framed by long black hair, Wang Xiating, age twenty-one, is a student from Hainan Island, the tropical paradise of the nouveau riche. She has a degree in hotel management. I am surprised to find a person with her qualifications underground. But Duoyou isn't; his years at university got him used to seeing students from the provinces inhabiting the entrails of the capital. When she was a student, Xiating had free lodgings on campus. Since starting work six months ago in a four-star hotel a twenty-minute walk from her room, she has been living underground, reduced to a rat-like existence despite her brilliant studies. From her salary of 3,000 yuan (US$425) a month, she spends 500 (US$70) on rent. Every other day, she works the night shift at the hotel and sleeps there, a real relief. She is spared the ordeal of a shower in a dark bathroom with a concrete floor covered in a thick layer of black filth, the white lather of her soap slipping over it. The smells of cooking and the heat that issue from the communal kitchen transform her relative cleanliness into something quite fleeting.

Suddenly, the terrible stench of an animal corpse fills the place.

"You smell that?" we all ask at once, covering our noses. "What is that stink?"

"You mean the smell of dead rat?" Xiating asks, a strange look on her face. "Someone must have left the door to the garbage room open. After you live here long enough, you don't smell anything anymore. But if you want to know the truth, I can't stand this place. You can't breathe. You have to line up to take a shower and make sure you have enough change to pay for hot water. Most of the time, I take a shower at the hotel. In the winter, it's too cold. And without daylight, and no windows, I get depressed. Some people manage to live here, but not me. I have to put up with it for five more months, until my internship is over. Then I'll go back to Hainan, and find a job in tourism."

But nearly a third of students who finish with diplomas do not find work in the year following graduation. And getting a university degree does not guarantee a higher salary. According to the National Bureau of Statistics, only three percent of young graduates find a job that offers a salary of more than 5,000 yuan (US$715). For seventy percent of those lucky enough to find work, the salary will top off at 2,000 yuan (US$285) a month—as much as a migrant worker makes. Because of the shortage of manpower in factories and on construction sites, the wages of migrant workers increased eighty percent between 2003 and 2009. During the same period, the starting salaries of young graduates stagnated. The failure rates in Chinese universities are so low that battalions of young graduates enter the job market each year, and there is fierce competition for every possible position. Despite the country's impressive growth over the last decade, the economy has not produced enough jobs to absorb the mass of young people, each holding a *gaokao* (the Chinese college entrance exam), plus another four or five years of university studies. A great number join the unemployment statistics right after graduation. According to an estimate that appeared in the Chinese press in 2014, the creation of 13 million additional jobs would be necessary to satisfy the increasing demand of the *daxuesheng shiye juntuan*, the army of unemployed graduates. A study by sociologist Lian Si revealed that, in Beijing alone, there are 150,000 "ants"—young graduates in search of work, or holding underpaid positions, and living in underground spaces. The same number applies to Shanghai. A million more ants inhabit basements and sub-basements in other big cities.

"Very few young people can change their destiny," says Hu Xingdou, economist at the Beijing Institute of Technology. "Even if they go to the large urban centers to improve their living conditions, they will still end up as part of the underclass. However, this community has an advantage: it is a lot more stubborn than most. The young rats—call them ants if you like—won't be the first to be affected by a slowdown in growth."

Tianmin, age twenty-two, and Qian, twenty-three, belong to that group of young university graduates. They arrived from Henan a few months ago. He trained as an engineer but has had to settle for a job as an IT technician. She has a diploma in Korean studies and found work in communications.

"I could have found a job that fits with my training in Zhengzhou, the capital of Henan," Tianmin says. The man with the boyish face is shirtless, wearing blue shorts as he soaps up his clothes on a wooden washboard in the concrete sink of the communal washroom. "But in Beijing, my IT job, though it takes less skill, is paid three times as much. For us new graduates, it's harder now to find work than it was ten years ago. Employers are very demanding because everyone has a university diploma nowadays. With all the economic development, there are plenty of opportunities in the big cities, but bosses would rather hire people with experience. Finding your first job is really an ordeal."

At the next sink, Qian, his girlfriend, is washing her hair and eyeing us hostilely. She's the one who insisted on moving to Beijing. She thought life in Henan was boring, and she wanted to see the world. The couple is renting a 12-square-meter (130-square-foot) room for 600 yuan (US$85) a month beneath the Zhujiang

Luzhou apartment complex in the Dingfuzhuang district, in the northeast part of the capital, next to the Beijing International Studies University. The Zhujiang Luzhou complex is made up of more than a dozen towers, each with its own subterranean labyrinth with more than sixty rooms. The network of hallways where Tianmin and Qian live has been graced with decoration: landscape paintings in the traditional Chinese style embellish the walls and a number carved from copper has been carefully affixed to each door. Even so, the couple tries to get out as often as possible. Sometimes they cook in their little space, but most of the time they eat out in one of the student restaurants in the area, where they put down 10 yuan (US$1.50) for a big bowl of noodles and twice that amount for a meat dish. Qian comes from a small city in Henan, where her parents have a grocery store. Tianmin, the son of peasants, was born in a village. If they find good jobs, both would prefer to stay in Beijing for five or six years, then return to Zhengzhou, where they first met in university.

"If you don't have *guanxi*, if your family doesn't have money, life can be hard in Beijing," Qian tells me, less tense about me being here now. "My parents are worried about me because I don't eat right and I don't sleep very well, but the basement is clean and not too damp. Before we came we knew that the conditions would be difficult. Honestly, I was expecting worse. If I had to spend the rest of my life like this, it would be terribly depressing. It's like back in the 1960s, the Middle Ages, except with internet. We won't be able to live in Beijing all our lives, because property simply costs too much. It's a good experience while we're young, but sooner or later, we'll have to leave. There's no other choice."

The couple have lived together for two years, and they are considering marriage. Tianmin would like to marry Qian next year, but his beloved is in no hurry to be tied down that quickly.

"She doesn't want to be a prisoner," Tianmin says sadly. "Qian considers her freedom before all else. No one can put her in a cage. I'll just have to be patient."

They agree on one thing: they won't have children. The abolition of the one-child restriction in 2015 didn't change anything for them.

Like a number of young people of their generation, who subscribe to a brand of individualism that didn't exist in China ten years earlier, Tianmin and Qian believe that the country is too polluted, the political climate too unstable, and the cost of living too high to raise children.

"With all these scandals with the food supply, I don't want to spend all my salary buying imported baby formula and organic stuff to keep from poisoning my kids," Tianmin says.

Every time I have conversations with young people, I am struck by the arguments they put forward against having children. The same perspective appears in any number of Western societies to a lesser degree, but I can't help thinking it is among the many catastrophes caused by the Chinese Communist Party, a perverse effect of its one-child policy and its obsession with development at any cost. Introduced in 1980, the one-child policy was meant to slow down the population explosion. This rule has been accused of creating an imbalance between the sexes and violence against women. Since the policy was instituted, the party has eased up on its much-criticized family planning regulations. The rules slowly relaxed to allow couples to have a second child if one of the partners was an only child. The measure was also eased for peasants, who could have a second child if the first was a girl, or if both partners were only children. Finally, in 2015, this unpopular law was abolished altogether, allowing all couples to have two children, since many Chinese economic experts and demographers warned that the aging population meant that great social and economic difficulties were looming in the future.

The abolition of the one-child policy has not delivered the surge in the birth rate that the country's authorities expected. A number of inquiries in the Chinese media have suggested that couples have gotten used to the one-child policy, and that very small apartments, the high cost of living, and the cost of education are hardly enticements to having a second child. The birth rate in China is declining, with 2018 producing the fewest babies since 1961, according to official records.

◆

Back at Julong Garden, where the rat tribe prospers beneath my feet, young Liu got married at twenty-four, pressured by his parents. They didn't want him to end up like all those other *diaosi* (literally, "dick hairs"), that generation of losers with depressive tendencies, with no wife or children or savings, and with a dead-end job paying nothing. But marital bliss didn't last long for Liu, who had no desire for children. He was pushed out by his in-laws only a few months after he married Weijia. His peasant parents, who hail from a village in the Jiangxi region in the southeast part of the country, had not succeeded in saving up enough money to pay for the wedding and set the couple up in life.

"When I was a kid, we were the first family in the village to have a TV," Liu remembers, sitting on a bottom bunk, wearing beige pants, a washed-out denim shirt, and ancient sneakers. "We were so proud. When I was fifteen, my father got sick and couldn't work, and my mother didn't have time to look after me. People didn't show their feelings where I lived, though sometimes my mother would ask me to forgive her for not spending more time with me. She would tell me to pay attention to what was on TV, since I had the chance to see what was happening in the outside world. When I turned twenty, my mother started pressuring me to find a wife, someone to take care of me, since I couldn't do it on my own."

Liu grew tired of his parents' harassment and left for Shanghai, where he joined the People's Liberation Army. His two years in the army were enough to convince him he wasn't soldier material, and in the end, he returned to the village to find a wife. The romanticism that Chinese people love to see in the movies is largely missing from real life. Outside of a few exceptions, marriage is a kind of contract by which two individuals pool their resources. The union is called *guorizi* (or "pass the days")—two people get together because life is easier that way. As he considered his options, Liu remembered Weijia, a classmate from high school, with whom he once had long conversations, and a certain understanding. During his leaves from the army, he would take her on little trips on his motorbike, her hair flowing in the wind as they traveled through golden fields of wheat. When he said one day that he'd like to meet her parents, she considered for a while, then said yes. This decision sealed their union, and they knew that marriage awaited them, but nothing was certain yet. According to tradition, Weijia's parents met his, and that's when the questioning started: "How many male children are there in your family?" "How much land does your family own?" "How many head of cattle will be in the dowry?" "Are you certain your daughter will get pregnant right away?"

Weijia's parents had one obsession: "Will Liu have built the house before the wedding?" Against their will, they gave in, and the wedding took place before the house was built. But the harassment stepped up. Both sets of parents pressured Liu to leave the village. His training as a software engineer would open the way for a fine career—but not in his native village.

"'Beijing, Beijing, you must go to Beijing. That's where every-thing happens. It's better for everyone if you go there.' My in-laws kept telling me that, all day long. Finally, I ended up packing my bags for Beijing," Liu remembers with a look of disgust.

The couple did not have children. His wife accompanied him to the station, where they said their farewells. A seventeen-hour train ride awaited him. That was two years ago. Today, the same seventeen hours separate him from his village, the fields he loved so much, the folk traditions, the spicy cuisine of his native region. He's returned to the village only twice, and Weijia has visited him in Beijing as many times. He still doesn't have the means to build the house. Tired of family pressures and long periods of separation, he is beginning to consider divorce.

Sitting on his bed, Liu smokes nervously as he tells his story, one that is so common. A dozen ashtrays are overflowing in this room that houses fourteen people. His comrades' dirty clothes are strewn on the floor, with plastic bowls of instant noodles lying next to them. Hangers attached to bunk beds and wires running across the 25-square meter (270-square-foot) room are used to keep the clean clothes clean. For washing their face and clothes everyone has a basin, which is stored under the bed when not in use. The room gives off an impressively virile odor. All fourteen comrades work in a neighboring restaurant, three of them in the kitchen, while the others do the dishes or wait on tables. The owner rents them this underground dormitory, from which they emerge only to go to work, seven days a week.

I ask one of the young men, wearing a black T-shirt transformed into leopard-print by a collection of stains, "Is the food good in your restaurant? Should I come and eat there some evening?"

"Of course—I'm the chef," he answers, gnawing away with great appetite at a piece of skin hanging from his thumb. "Come and we'll cook you up a feast you won't forget."

"Is your kitchen as well maintained as your room?"

In return, I get the silent treatment. The chef offers his hand covered in black scabs, then takes his leave. I never found the courage to try their restaurant.

"Sure, life isn't easy," Liu admits. "It's not just the lack of light that's depressing; it's the smell, the mess, the lack of privacy. It's embarrassing to bring a girl back. When Weijia came, it was complicated. She never liked Beijing, and there was no way she would come here and be with me. But despite the problems, I've found a new life here, and I wouldn't be able to stand the village again. Here, you can meet people from all different horizons, even in the basements. There's culture, books, films, theater, museums. You can even talk with foreigners."

Liu is about to leave the entrails of the city and its vampires, and enter the world of light among the living. He found work with a cultural association for the development of Buddhism thanks to a customer at the restaurant.

"The job doesn't exactly fit my training as an IT engineer," he notes, "but the salary is good enough for me to live in a normal apartment. I did a little research and the prospects are exciting. The company that hired me restored an old Buddhist temple so people can worship their ancestors. They can buy a spot to put their ashes. The whole thing is for corrupt rich people who want to try and save their souls. They've got a heavy burden on their conscience, all those people who got rich on the backs of the rat people. They sit at the wheel of their BMWs, or their Audis or Mercedes, and they work in fancy glass towers built by workers who live like animals underground, without hope for a better life."

Despite the posters on the walls, the governments that have followed Deng Xiaoping have not distinguished themselves with their sense of social responsibility. Success and wealth have become such an obsession that many Chinese will do anything to get ahead. The perspective of his new job has given Liu a sense of adventure, and he doesn't intend to stop there. He wants to stay in Beijing another two or three years, then head for a foreign country.

"I'd like to live in Finland or the United States," he declares, like a kid in a candy store. "I want to see whether life is better there than here. I've read a lot of articles online about the different countries in the world, but with censorship, and government manipulation, you never know if you can trust what you read. Some things seem completely unreasonable."

"Can you give me an example?"

"Well, it might sound silly," he says, a little embarrassed, "but I read that in Australia, men and women split the bill when they go to a restaurant. That seems unlikely, considering how much money men have there. I think that's just misinformation to damage Australia's image."

The government's control of information is so strict that many Chinese people don't know how to separate truth from lies, especially when it comes to online sources. The result is a form of paranoia, often senseless and difficult to control, set off by actual facts. On the Chinese internet, information judged "sensitive" is deleted right before users' eyes, especially when it refers to an event that discredits the government. Liu would be speechless to learn that in many countries women often split the bill, and sometimes even pick up the tab entirely. Imagine his shock if I tried to convince him that it is socially unacceptable for men to come on to women in Germany, where women generally make the first move according to their desires.

CHAPTER 8

THE *MINGONG*: EMPIRE BUILDERS

A t the time of the emperors, Beijing erected walls and guard towers to protect the Northern Capital from hordes of invaders. In the twenty-first century, it is building ring roads, stretching ever farther afield, gobbling up agricultural land and green spaces. Steam shovels, road graders, and cement mixers are in frenetic action near Langfang, a city halfway between Beijing and Tianjin, its giant neighbor in Hebei province. The 1,000 kilometers (620 miles) of the 7th Ring Road orbit so far from the center of the capital that most of its route moves through neighboring Hebei province, passing through Chengde, the former summer residence of the emperors. Some sections are as far as 175 kilometers (nearly 110 miles) from the glass and steel towers of the Beijing Central Business District. The 7th Ring Road is emblematic of today's Chinese megacities, dominated by the car, and the 8th Ring Road is a highway that runs entirely outside Beijing municipality. This frenzied construction, and the speed at which the city is devouring rural districts, is enough to make your head spin. Chinese urban centers can crush you with their density and immense size. The country is losing part of its soul in its accelerated development toward twenty-first-century gianthood. But no new identity has emerged, since the Communist Party prevents society from evolving in new directions.

There is no equivalent in history to the speed at which the most populous country in the world is changing. Ready for any task, on the margins socially and administratively, the *mingong* have been the cornerstone of this process.

"Without them, these megacities would have never been built so quickly," points out Zhou Haiwang from the Shanghai Academy of Social Sciences.

These rural migrants have increased the urban population by 500 million, with a double effect on the economy. Their salaries allow them to participate in mass consumption, and they also add to growth and inject money into the cities. Their flow into urban centers brings an abundant workforce, creating fierce competition on the job market, which pushes salaries down, with the result that a megacity can emerge and develop at very low cost. As of 2019, China has more than 160 metropolitan centers with populations of more than a million people, and the number keeps rising. Of the world's thirty-three megacities (more than 10 million inhabitants), in 2019, seven were found in the People's Republic: Shanghai (24.2 million), Beijing (21.5 million), Chongqing (approximately 30 million with its twenty-five districts), Tianjin (15.6 million), Guangzhou (14.9 million), Shenzhen (12.5 million), and Wuhan (11 million). And on it goes … Another dozen cities boast populations just under 10 million.

The shiny skyscrapers, the ultramodern airports, the skeins of bridges and elevated expressways, the flamboyant shopping centers where crowds of young people infatuated with new technologies are busy wiping away the country's agrarian past. In Beijing, the dazzling towers of the CBD are the showroom of this new soulless empire obsessed with money. Built on 4 square kilometers (1.5 square miles) in the heart of the Chaoyang district, between the 3rd and 4th Ring Roads, the zone is ever-expanding and has taken over as one of the major financial centers of the country, attracting 117 Fortune 500 companies, including media and information technology. More than sixty percent of foreign businesses that have set up shop in Beijing have their main offices there.

Compared to twentieth-century architecture, with its austere and often Soviet style, the Chinese megacity has, over recent decades, displayed innovation to go along with the explosion in property development and urban sprawl. These are ideal conditions for attracting architects from all over the world, well-known names like Jean Nouvel, as well as a good number of young unknowns, who have seized opportunities in China they would have never seen in their home countries in the early stages of their careers. The gentle oval curves of the late Iraqi British architect Zaha Hadid, whose structures can be seen all across the capital, have altered the Beijing horizon with a new look.

Rather overwhelmed by all this modernity, and trying to impose the Stalinist aesthetic, President Xi Jinping called for an end to "weird architecture" in a country where there is no end to urban curiosities. A great admirer of Mao Zedong, and the most powerful Chinese leader since the Great Helmsman, Uncle Xi can't stop himself from wanting to control everything, including cultural production and the new face of the cities. His comments set off an avalanche of reaction on local social media. "Is someone trying to impose one sense of aesthetics on millions of people?" a Weibo user wondered. Xi based his opinions on the public debate over a few new buildings. It all started with the new headquarters of state television network CCTV in Beijing, designed by Dutch architect Rem Koolhaas—all 234 meters (nearly 770 feet) and fifty-one floors of it—which unleashed a torrent of sarcasm, its shape earning it the popular nickname "big pants." The *People's Daily* echoed Xi's rigid judgment, yet the newspaper's headquarters—a strangely shaped tower in Beijing generally considered to be phallic—was so roundly mocked on social media that the censors banned all discussion on the topic for a period of time.

Real estate developers were not impressed by the Chinese leader's comments on aesthetics, so the CBD keeps spreading. Tower III of the China World Trade Center—all 330 meters (almost 1,100 feet), eighty-one floors, and thirty elevators—dominates the district with its silvery glow. It is home to the Atmosphere Bar, the highest in the city, on the eightieth floor, where you can sip one of the 300 cocktails as you take in the view, stretching from Tiananmen Square, the heart of Communist power, to the mountains beyond.

In the upscale neighborhood of Sanlitun, a stone's throw from the CBD, the silver towers with their blue highlights, courtesy of the Soho developers, dazzle passersby. Dozens of workers, their yellow hard hats under their arms, enjoy the last rays of sunlight and clear sky, a rare luxury in a place where sheets of pollution weigh upon the atmosphere two-thirds of the year. It is six in the evening and the *mingong*, with their dirt-streaked faces, are about to eat their meal at the work site canteen, now that their long day's labor is over. They are part of the construction crew for a new skyscraper, 150 meters (nearly 500 feet) tall, which will hold an international luxury hotel and a shopping concourse. In

Changsha, the capital of Hunan province, where Mao Zedong studied and discovered Communism, China has shown it can make a fifty-seven-story tower sprout out of the ground in nineteen days, thanks to 12,000 workers.

From my Sanlitun office, I watched with some impatience as work progressed on a new, sail-shaped glass tower. When I first came to Beijing in 2013, I liked the idea of seeing the building grow before my very eyes, outside my window, like the barometer of the country's economic growth. But then, as growth "fell" to only seven percent, I ended up with a three-year-long show. Teams of hundreds of workers spelled each other off to push the project toward its conclusion, but glitches large and small slowed it down. One month, I looked on as, over a period of several days, the workers removed the glass facade that they had spent weeks putting into place—the panels were oriented in the wrong direction.

The workers who built that international hotel were the elite of the *mingong*. Coddled by their bosses, they were put up in comfortable prefab work site barracks with balconies, located between the Soho towers and Workers' Stadium. Aware of their good luck, they were in no hurry to criticize their working conditions.

"Of course we all know how fortunate we are to be working on this project," says one of them, a twenty-one-year-old man fresh from Gansu province. "It's my first job. I work from eight in the morning to six in the evening. So far it's been two months, and my starting salary is 5,000 yuan [US$715]. The conditions are pretty good. The lodging and the food are decent. My job is installing the air-conditioning system. I know I have at least six months' work ahead of me. Then I'll wait for my company to send me to another site. It might be in Beijing, but it could just as well be in Shenzhen or Guangzhou. It doesn't matter. Anything is okay. I want to see the world."

The young man has red cheeks and a baby face not yet marked by years of work, and his comrades have an affectionate nickname for him: *baozi*, or "dumpling face." He is following in the footsteps of his father, who worked for twenty years on construction sites in the biggest Chinese cities, and then returned to his Gansu village to open a grocery store. He was employed by the giant BTP Group, and when he left for his village, to be reunited with his wife, he recommended his son to his boss. In China, on every level, to get the best spot, you need *guanxi*. But some men who have worked for this company for several years don't mind admitting that they're tired of it. They are nomads, moving from site to site, and living in barracks, even comfortable ones, wears them down in the end. Separated from their families all year long, immersed in solitude with no emotional outlet, they work seven days a week and are often summoned back in the evening for overtime.

◆

The People's Republic is being shaken by twenty-first century social problems caused by nineteenth-century conditions: poverty, medieval working conditions, corrupt management. According to China Labour Bulletin, based in Hong Kong, more than eighty percent of migrant workers employed in construction have not signed work contracts, and in some cities, such as Chongqing, Zhengzhou, and Wuhan, that figure can rise to ninety percent. But even those who have signed a contract are not given a copy to refer to in case of conflict. Workers are often injured but a good number of injured men never receive any compensation, or if they do, it is a meager sum. Eighty percent of *mingong* are forced to settle their demands outside of a court, and they receive a fifth of the compensation they would have been awarded had they been able to undertake legal proceedings. The less skilled workers, especially those over fifty-five, are the most vulnerable, and given the most dangerous jobs. It is common to see men who look like grandpas hanging from crude wooden swings, held in place by old ropes, busy washing skyscraper windows high above the street. Some fall to their deaths when the worn ropes give way. Often, their bosses refuse to pay compensation to the widows left behind in villages with no means of survival. The companies often claim that the men were negligent when they rigged up their positions.

Revolts have grown more frequent. With 1,379 social conflicts in 2014, the number of protests has multiplied threefold in three years, according to China Labour Bulletin. With 650 million citizens online, the internet has played an enormous role in mobilizing digital dissidents who denounce corrupt bosses, protected by shady local party directors. One site is dedicated exclusively to denouncing the luxury watches worn by party members. An emblematic case concerns Comrade Watchband, a local comrade from the Shanxi region, who liked to exhibit watches on his wrist worth several years' salary. The investigators from the party's Central Commission for Discipline Inspection, tasked with fighting corruption, discovered that this comrade had property worth 4.8 million yuan (US$688,800), whereas his monthly salary stood at 8,000 yuan (US$1,150). He was sentenced to fourteen years in prison. Although the digital dissidents sometimes succeed in knocking a few corrupt party leaders off their pedestals, they are rarely able to create meaningful improvements in working conditions.

◆

Jian, forty years old, trained and apprenticed in construction in Henan, but the work was too sporadic and the pay too meager in his home province, so in 2005 he headed for Beijing. There, he helped erect buildings on the famous Chang'an Avenue, the avenue of eternal peace, an artery that runs through the city from east to west, past Tiananmen Square and the Forbidden City, the nerve center of political power.

"I am very proud to have taken part in such prestigious projects," says this giant of a man with steel false teeth. "I'm very lucky to live at a time like this, because there's a lot of building everywhere. There's no lack of work. We're building tomorrow's China. I hope the country will go on developing in a stable, prosperous way. That's our priority."

For the first years, he lived in underground dormitories rented out by his bosses, located near the job sites. When his family joined him in 2010, Jian rented a 15-square-meter (160-square-foot) room underground in the center of the city. His wife found a job as a building superintendent, which meant they could then live in the little apartment that came with her position, with a window vent and an additional 5-square-meter (almost 50-square-foot) room, where their daughter, glued to the TV, ingests high doses of cartoons. The couple saves on the rent, which becomes a kind of salary. Meanwhile, Jian brings in 8,000 yuan (US$1,150) a month as a construction foreman.

"With the little window, we get some fresh air. That's good for our daughter's health," he explains, scratching at a piece of dried food on his checked shirt. "She's outside all day at day care. She only spends her nights and weekends here."

His criteria for his daughter's health are quite different from those of the people who live on the surface, concerned as they are with air pollution and how to escape it. To spur its development, China consumes half the world's coal and derives seventy percent of its energy from it. Air pollution has become one of the population's main sources of discontent. People are tired of suffocating and hearing statistics about the exploding rates of lung cancer in urban areas. The citizens of Beijing all have their masks and air purifiers to try to protect their lungs and bronchial tubes. The office buildings and upper-class residences, like the one Jian is building, come with air-conditioning and filtration systems. In Beijing, the density of fine particles in the air is above the levels recommended by the World Health Organization two-thirds of the year. During one particularly heavy "airpocalyptic" episode in January 2014, the density of particles measuring 2.5 microns in diameter, the most dangerous kind, reached the threshold of 671 micrograms per cubic meter, according to the American embassy—a level twenty-six times higher than the limit recommended for twenty-four-hour exposure. This pea soup of pollution means that cars have their headlights on at noon. The skyscrapers disappear into the smog. The particular smell of burned coal and chemical fog fills the nostrils. My son, Antoine, is crazy about sports, but he has to spend long hours inside after school is over, looking out the window. As he breathes purified air, he gazes upon the gray atmosphere in disgust. His racing bike hangs from hooks in his room, unusable. Meanwhile, Jian's daughter has no choice but to breathe in the pollution, which will reduce her life expectancy by several years.

His five-year-old daughter is in day care, but next year, the thorny question of her school registration will come up. Since Jian doesn't have a *hukou* for Beijing, like all the *mingong* living in the capital, he lacks the papers needed to sign her up for public school. And a private establishment is way beyond his means.

"We'll have to send her back to the village next year, so she can stay with my parents," he says, with a sad smile that displays his steel teeth. "Unfortunately, they're probably too old to take care of her. Most likely my wife will have to go with her, and we'll be separated. It's unfair. In Beijing, we could have a brilliant future, full of opportunities, but we can't stay together as a family because we have no *hukou*. I have no benefits, no chance for my daughter to go to school, no affordable health care. The *mingong* who work in construction contribute more to Beijing than the people who were born here. We give more to this place than they do and we get nothing back."

A second-class citizen, Jian tries to rationalize the injustice of his situation. For his family, a return to the countryside, and a better environment, will probably be better for their health.

"One day, I'll go back to the village to get away from the pollution," he swears.

According to Lu Huitin, a sociology professor at Peking University, China has leaned on this source of cheap labor for thirty years without offering anything in return. And the system is beginning to reach its limits.

"Human beings mean nothing to the state," he says. "The country is already running on the second generation of *mingong* who have been sacrificed. Everyone knows this system can't survive in the long term. The *mingong* want to build their lives in the cities with their families, but they can't because of all the obstacles. Too many obstacles. This contradiction has to be resolved. The gap is too wide between their dreams, their reality, and the government's rules. The second generation's demands are more forceful. They want to stay in the cities."

◆

In the district of Beijing known as Chaoyangmen Nei, a few meters' distance from the Galaxy SOHO, the most distinctive shopping center in Beijing, designed by the famous architect Zaha Hadid, Zhao is waiting for us in his stained work clothes and hard hat. It is six in the evening and he has finished his day's work installing the elevators in a fourteen-story building. Small, slim but ropy, his eyes attentive, Zhao is sure that these will be high-class, luxury offices.

"Not only are they putting in ten elevators for a fourteen-floor building, they're Japanese elevators. Super-luxury," he states, and he should know: he is running a team of a dozen specialized technicians.

His employer found him a hole in the second sub-basement of a good building in this quickly developing district in the city center. His labyrinth looks something like a submarine. To reach his room, he has to travel down narrow tubes illuminated by fluorescent lights, past blue and white walls, and then go through two flood chambers fitted with heavy metal doors. When he opens the entrance to his room, where two of his colleagues are waiting, a dense cloud of steam escapes. Zhao pushes us inside.

"Quick, they're making some grub," he tells me, motioning to the electric wok, where tripe is sizzling with vegetables and chilies. "We're not allowed to cook. If the underground boss catches us, he'll fine us."

"What do you mean, fine you? Is he hitting you up for money for the city or for the owner?" I ask in my naivete.

"How long have you lived in China?" Zhao asks, laughing under his hard hat. "Don't you know how it works here? You saw that guy in the glass cage on the way in—he keeps an eye on everyone coming and going. He's the superintendent, and he's the spy. We call him the 'boss.' If he catches us cooking, we slip him some money, 200 or 500 yuan [US$30–70] depending on his mood. He pockets the money, and he won't rat us out to the man who owns these rooms. That way, we won't get kicked out for breaking the rules. Everything in this country runs on bribes. To get a promotion at work, you have to pay off your superior. If you make a mistake on the site, you can fix it with an envelope. The rich pay so their kids will get good grades at school and get into a good university. That way they'll know the right people and have the money to get the best jobs."

Zhao was twenty-three when he left his village in the coastal province of Jiangsu, where his peasant parents grew sorghum. The children of the families he knew decided to leave their farms for a factory in the region, one of the industrial powerhouses of the country. But not him—he had other ambitions.

"Factory wages are too low," he explains, as he slips his cell phone onto the charger hanging from the end of a naked wire. He takes a drink of water. "The salary is just enough to survive on. You can't save anything. I wanted more."

After getting specialized training in elevator installation in 2000, Zhao headed for Beijing, where he found work right away. He stayed until 2008, and then moved to Shenzhen, the cradle of Deng Xiaoping's economic opening, at the far end of the delta of the Pearl River in Guangdong province. He figured the property boom would be stronger there, in the mushrooming urban area across from Hong Kong, but he didn't last long. The madness of unchecked urban development in the world's factory belt was too much for him.

"In Shenzhen, the bosses make the workers labor in their factories until they drop dead. You have to sleep there. And then, you only sleep a few hours a night and work seven days a week. So the developers want to do the same. They run construction day and night so the building goes up faster, but there's always someone missing, and they put pressure on you to replace him. Sooner or later, you end up making a mistake. Two years later, I moved to Jinan, in Shandong province, but there wasn't enough to do there. When a friend recommended me for a job in Beijing, I jumped on it."

At the head of a small team of twelve technicians, Zhao works from seven in the morning to six in the evening, seven days a week, for a monthly salary of 8,000 yuan (US$1,150). After the job is over, the men return to their basements, where they sleep five to a room. Zhao has a double bed in the rear, right-hand corner. The walls are papered with pouting red lips and shapely legs in a patchwork of giant advertising posters for ladies' beauty products. Two clothes wires are stretched from the pipes that run along the ceiling to a metal bunk bed. A few pairs of underwear, socks, and undershirts dry there. Every man has his own night table covered in ashtrays overflowing with butts, packs of local cigarettes, water bottles, cell phones, and chargers. No TV, no closets. The men don't have a single set of street clothes: no shirt, no pants, no street shoes or sneakers.

Half-admiring, half-pitying, I tell him, "You live like monks here!"

"Not exactly," he corrects me. "We're poorer than the Taoists and the Buddhists. We're at the bottom of the social ladder. We could buy a television, but we move every two months. What would we do with it? At first, I had more stuff. Then I got sick of having to carry everything around with me. All the *mingong* live like this. If I want to look at the news, I go to the park. With my smartphone, I can pirate the Wi-Fi of people who live on the surface. That's how I talk to my wife and son, and I can see them on video. She shows me pictures of the village. When we want to have some fun, we go to the karaoke. But that doesn't happen more than three times a year, because I don't like to drink, and it costs money."

His wife and eleven-year-old son live in his village. She is breaking her back in a textile factory from dawn to dusk and doesn't have time to raise their child. The grandparents look after him. Zhao visits them in the village three times a year, for a dozen days or so. A little bit embarrassed in front of his colleagues, he admits that loneliness is a source of pain. One of his buddies, who is lying on his bed, wearing only a pair of underpants, listens avidly, chain-smoking "to keep the mosquitoes away," while two other men rush from one end of the room to the other, trying to kill insects with their hands. Every six-legged corpse sets off a victory cry and a wide, satisfied smile.

"But you talk to your son all the time," the man on the bed says.

"There are so many things I'd like to tell him," Zhao says. "But he only listens for a few seconds and never gives me more than a yes or no answer. Most of the time he won't even take the phone to talk to me. The truth is, I abandoned him. The boy grew up without a father, and I'm a stranger to him. My parents are too old for the job. They don't know how to control him. He's very hard to handle. My wife and son come here once a year, in the summer. I take them to see Tiananmen Square, the Forbidden City, the Great Wall, the museums, the *hutong*. But they can't stay more than a week, because we have to go to a hotel, and I have to ask for days off to take care of them."

Zhao dreams of a different life, of returning to the village to care for his son and share experiences with him. He admits he doesn't care for the anonymous, soulless existence of the big cities and prefers the villages, where everyone knows each other, where people talk and help each other out. A builder of tomorrow's China, he does say he feels proud when he goes by the thirty-story glass towers of the CBD—he installed their elevators.

"But I know I'm missing the best years of my family life," he says, as he flips through photographs of his wife and son and village on his phone. His wife, her short hair framing a pretty face, wears a faraway smile. And his son has the hostile look of a boy who doesn't want to have his picture taken because he has better things to do.

"It's like they've been stolen from me, but I had no choice. It's not fair. I'll have to save at least 500,000 yuan [over US$70,000] to marry off my son. And that's just to finance the house, not pay for the wedding supper. In Beijing, the salaries are higher, but so is the cost of living. Sometimes I can put a few yuan aside. In the cities around my village, there's no work for me in elevators. I'd have to settle for a less-skilled job, and the pay would be a lot less in one of the local factories.

"Okay, so I'm part of the country's economic development. In 2002, I was hardly making twenty yuan [three dollars] a day. Every year, my salary has gone up, but so have my boss's demands and the volume of work. Us *mingong* are the ones who have least benefited from growth. The real winners are the rich. And the rich are getting richer while we stand still. I can't hope for more for my children because the social elevator doesn't work in this country. You need *guanxi* and little red envelopes if you want to get ahead."

"It's only a matter of time before China becomes the most important economic power in the world," believes sociology professor Lu Huitin. "But if we don't solve the *mingong* problem, there will be no sustainable development. If their living conditions don't progress, they will have no buying power, and growth will continue to swell, but artificially. China must move from being the world's factory to the world's laboratory of innovation, if prosperity is to continue long term. For that, we will need ultra-skilled workers, like in Germany. But bosses don't encourage the *mingong* to become more skilled; they don't give them any rights. The ultimate goal of growth is to offer a better life to the greatest number and develop a modern society. At the same time, we are seeing the negative impact of growth on the environment. Without a solution, we will have social problems. Without social justice, prosperity is not sustainable."

Zhao doesn't believe he'll ever see a *mingong* revolt. After fifteen years, the men, worn down by their work in the big cities, have one idea in mind: return to their villages. But there are very few of them who can make that move before the age of fifty-five or sixty. The countryside is full of millions of people, living virtually pennilessly, who dream of taking their place. They think the *mingong* are very well off, with their nice clothes, the latest model smartphones, their houses in the village, and their cars.

Living far from his family for years now, nearly forty, Zhao hopes to return to his village. His desire has recently become stronger. His wife is three months pregnant with their second child. Zhao does not know the gender of his future offspring, and it will determine the rest of his existence. He burns small paper offerings in front of Buddha statues to try to influence the outcome.

"I'm very happy to be a father again," he says. "But I'm just praying for the child to be a girl. A second boy would be a sentence to eternal poverty. I would have to work to my dying day to pay for a second dowry. But I have no illusions. Poor people attract poverty and make more boys than girls."

CHAPTER 9

A NIGHT WITH THE RATS

When I was a teenager, sleepover invitations to friends' houses always caused a certain amount of anxiety. I grew up partly in the United States, where the practice was a lot more common than in France. Sleepover invitations happened just about every weekend. At the time, the list of things I was willing to eat was very short. The menus that my friends' parents dished up gave me the shivers.

I feel that same apprehension with each new assignment in a foreign country, more fleetingly, in the first few minutes when I find myself alone in a hotel room. That feeling is impossible to fight, whether I'm being sent to cover the conflict in a war-torn land or the German elections.

But I have never felt such a mixture of trepidation and excitement as when I cross paths with Zheng in the walkway outside of Julong in the morning, and he tells me, "Tonight is the night. My wife went back to the village for a few days. Her mother is sick. She's old—I think the end is near. You can take her place in the bunk bed."

I had planned to have dinner with two friends, since I was alone, with summer vacation on. We had our eye on an Italian restaurant in the *hutong*, the traditional Beijing quarter, a couple of steps from the Drum Tower, which rang out the hours in the time of the emperors. I was already dreaming of the handmade pasta cooked to perfection, washed down with a Vino Nobile, and followed with a plate of cheeses imported from Italy. The outdoor part of the little trattoria, lit by candles, looks onto a narrow passage that has all the charm of traditional Beijing life, such as it has been preserved in a few special spots in the capital, far from the modern districts, with their impersonal concrete towers that, little by little, have killed off any sense of social life. Electric rickshaws move through the humid night with their characteristic high-pitched hum. Shirtless grandfathers step out to take in the air and smoke a cigarette as grandmothers in pajamas preside over their grandchildren peeing in the gutter. Friendly glances are exchanged, then a few bits of conversation, and with the evening comes the feeling of having shared something of China. Without ever having to leave our European comfort level, of course.

When we return to our neighborhood by bike, through the *hutong*, my wife, Laetitia, and I almost always stop in one of those miniscule Beijing taverns for a nightcap. Those places are so small you can't help but be social. A few minutes later, the Chinese customers are all over us, taking selfies on their smartphones, and the conversation is off and running, in broken Chinese or English, spontaneous, with no taboos, and full of laughter. After a few confessions about our hopes and dreams around a round of Yanjings, the beer of Beijing, we head home

A Night with the Rats

with the feeling that we just might have understood something about the Chinese. On the way, we pedal in silence, as if to preserve the magic of the moment, because the next day, I am just as overwhelmed as before by the map of the country hanging on my office wall. China is so enormous and diverse, despite the superficial uniformity forced on it by Communism. Discovering it is an inexhaustible search; a person would need a lifetime.

◆

Now here I am, trapped for the evening. I picture myself hanging on to my smartphone translator in a gloomy basement, sleeping amid the smells of piss and mold, the sounds of men clearing their throats, a few feet from my bed. Maybe I'm not really made for this immersive kind of investigation, even in the short term. It takes a form of self-denial that I really don't have. But I've gone too far and accepted the invitation, though a little unwillingly. I run to the supermarket to buy a bottle of *baijiu*, sorghum alcohol with devastating effects. I choose a midrange brand, hoping it won't be out of place with what the people beneath my feet are used to drinking. I slip it into my little knapsack with two liter bottles of water, a few toiletries, a flashlight, and some flip-flops to protect me on the trip to the toilet.

Zheng told me to show up at six. He is standing in front of the entrance to Building 7. The elevator isn't working, so we take the darkened stairway. Not a single light bulb is working. When we reach the second basement, I discover the harsh white light, the dark corners where cockroaches thrive, and the smell that grabs me by the throat. Zheng is used to all this, and he is in a splendid mood. Bare clotheslines add to the sinister atmosphere— the rat people's clothes have disappeared, and so has all the life in this virtually deserted chamber. The silence is broken only by the crackling of fluorescent lights.

The dormitory that used to be filled with cleaning ladies employed by the bars at the Workers' Stadium is empty. They disappeared overnight without anyone knowing whether their boss found them another more affordable spot or they all got fired together. The *mingong* with the dirty faces have folded up their tents as well. Their construction project is finished, and they have migrated elsewhere in town, or maybe to the far end of the country. The atmosphere is sad underground, empty but for the employees of the residence above. An intolerable odor of excrement and ammonia lies heavy over the place.

I put my bag in his room and wait for Zheng, who has gone to walk the dogs that belong to a rich Chinese couple in the building. Sitting by myself on the bunk bed, lit by a small lamp sending out a yellowish glow, I am awash in doubt and disappointment. I was hoping to strengthen ties with the inhabitants of the underground, discover their ways, and find out a little more about their lives. But now I'm trapped for the evening in an empty labyrinth.

◆

When he comes back, Zheng leads me into the kitchen, where two of his neighbors are making dinner. They have seen me prowling around the hallways for months now, and they don't react. I remember the festive atmosphere from my first visit to the kitchen, for New Year. This time, the welcome is not so warm; the spontaneous effect of my first appearance has worn off. Zheng opens a Tsingtao and pours two glasses of beer. We toast each other, then drain our glasses. Sitting on a child-sized chair, he cleans spinach and black mushrooms, tosses them into a wok with pieces of chicken and peanuts, then adds a splash of vinegar. His neighbors have already moved on by the time we sit down to dinner at the little Formica table. We toast a second time with our short glasses of beer, then devour the meal. Zheng eats noisily with his bowl under his chin, pushing rice and vegetables with his chopsticks. He is exhausted by his hard day's work and not very talkative. Our attempts at conversation are whittled down to a few comments about the meal and the smallness of the room. I am sorry I came without Duoyou, who would have improved the atmosphere, and whose linguistic expertise would have allowed us to have a real conversation. Here, our exchanges reach their limit even faster than during our first dinner. I wait for the end of the meal before producing my bottle of *baijiu*. We knock back a few glasses, toasting our friendship as we clear and wash the dishes. Then we head toward the room.

I feel I made a mistake by bringing the bottle. When we go into the dormitory, I see that Zheng's roommates have turned off the light and are sleeping. The *baijiu* has literally dried me up. Terribly thirsty, I drain the first liter of water, even knowing it means I'll have to make a trip to the toilet. I lie down on the top bunk with my flashlight. The springs squeal with every move I make. Zheng turns off his light after wishing me good night. Wrapped in the dank warmth that feels almost viscous, I lie motionless. We fall asleep a minute later. I wake up at three a.m., thirsty, my skull pounding with the painful pulse of *baijiu*. I switch on my flashlight, keeping my hand over the end to dim the light, and search for the second bottle of water. I empty it, but my thirst remains unslaked. The bunk bed rattles as I climb down to make the trip to the toilet. I hold my breath, the only defense against the stinking air. Nausea clings to me like a film, and sleep is impossible after that. Powerful snoring shakes the room. I doze until morning, dreaming of the shower that awaits me a couple stories up, and my bed, and a cold Coke. At 5:30, Zheng's alarm clock sets me free. A migraine is the excuse I use to go home and take an aspirin, and I am spared the ordeal of garlicky noodles for breakfast. I wish Zheng a good day, discouraged by this missed opportunity. He waves goodbye with his usual smile.

Back in the comfort of my apartment, I breathe in the air that is wonderfully cool, thanks to climate control. After a lengthy shower, I make a good strong coffee. I have to admit: I'm relieved at having escaped that claustrophobic world. But I'm also sorry that most of the inhabitants disappeared so suddenly, for they had turned the underground into a lively place. True, I deserted too quickly this morning. Even if I do know there would probably have been nothing exciting about watching Zheng do his ablutions and swallow down a quick breakfast. I succeeded in crossing a barrier, and being accepted into the world of the rats, but the experiment ended too quickly.

CHAPTER 10

KINGS AND KINGLETS AMONG THE RATS

Her plush outfit, pink heading toward fuchsia, is the latest trend for people living on the surface. Her plastic flip-flops and nail polish are color coordinated. Short and stout, with power and determination, she bears down on us. We are hiding in the common bathroom beneath the Zhujiang Luzhou apartment complex, in the Dingfuzhuang district, near the Beijing International Studies University, where we came to talk to the young residents. She spotted us thanks to her surveillance cameras posted in the labyrinth, where she rents out some sixty rooms.

"I'm the queen here," she declares, looking like a nightmare version of Barbie. "No one is allowed to talk to the residents."

"This is the first I've heard of that," I say, knowing I'll never get her to change her mind; she has decided to expel us. "We were invited by friends. Can't they have visitors?"

"I'm the queen. I say what's what," she decrees, her perm shaking like a Marie Antoinette wig. "You're bothering people with all your questions. Everything goes through me. If you wanted to talk to someone, you should have asked my permission first. Now it's too late. Anyway, I would have said no, because it's not allowed."

"Who says it's not allowed, and why?"

"The local government doesn't let foreigners visit the underground rooms and talk to the people who live here," the queen informs me. "The people who live here aren't happy to be in these conditions, but they don't have a choice. They don't have the means to go anywhere else. It's not a good solution, but everyone gets something out of it. But you foreigners try to make everything look bad, to weaken China."

"This is reality. We're just trying to understand it better."

"Get out of here now!" she hollers, pushing us toward the exit stairway. "Go back where you came from—you know the way. You're not wanted here. Go stir up shit in your own country and leave us alone."

Like many Westerners, I entertain the illusion that globalization, and the fact that I buy products made in China, creating millions of factory jobs in the process, gives me some vague moral right. My illusion quickly goes up in smoke, and I feel more like a voyeur. The queen slams the heavy metal door in our faces with a great crash. She belongs to a class of her own—the ones who rent out the underground, who build up comfortable nest eggs but go on living in the entrails of the city to manage the rentals and make sure the tenants respect the rules. The slightest infraction, punishable by a fine, adds to her revenue. These queens, kings, and kinglets are the main obstacles to our research. Afraid that bad press will lead to the "administrative shutdown" of their locales, they close a curtain of discretion around their shady business.

Liu Qing, one such landlord, whom I met through connections with an architect, agreed to give us a few details about how the underground is rented. Dressed in washed-out Italian jeans, a black T-shirt, and a green-and-yellow jacket from the Beijing soccer club, he rents out thirty or so rooms in the basement of the Huajiadi residence, in the city center. The average monthly fee is 700 yuan (US$100), which adds up to a yearly revenue of 252,000 yuan (US$36,000). From that amount, he must deduct 25,000 yuan (US$3,550) that he pays the local government for the right to exploit the basement, and for small repairs. He has lived underneath the Huajiadi building for six years, and spends the greater part of his time smoking cigarettes and surfing the web as he keeps watch over the security cameras. He makes regular rounds to ensure his tenants aren't committing some infraction. He tries to catch them in the act, but his shuffling steps and the characteristic sound of his white hospital shoes quickly tip off the rats.

"I have to live here," he tells me with a pinched expression. "Otherwise, I'd need to hire a guard and my business wouldn't be profitable."

◆

Zhou Zishu, a young architect, carried out a project in Huajiadi aimed at making underground lodging in Beijing more livable. With funds he gathered from former rats who had succeeded in business, Zhou repainted the hallways and rooms, installed a new ventilation system, and outfitted the rooms with wooden furniture and a place to watch movies, along with a common space for cultural exchange, including meetings between those who live on the surface and the others who live beneath it. When we returned to the residence a few months later to attend one such event, we found the door locked. A paper with the stamp of the civil defense department declared the area closed for security reasons.

"Liu Qing was a real swindler," Zhou lamented. "It was supposed to serve as a model for all Beijing. We signed a two-year contract, but he didn't even have permission to rent out the space. I lost everything. He took the money and ran. I don't even know where he is now."

To protect the capital city in case of Soviet bombardment, legislation was passed that made it obligatory for every new building put up in the 1960s to have an underground shelter. It would belong to the Chinese state and be managed by the civil defense department. For a certain sum, the administration would authorize commercial use, but over the last few months, it ordered the shutdown of dozens of the most outdated or dangerous locations. The authorities keep an eye on the state of the ventilation systems, the electrical setup, and anti-flood measures, such as airlocks like in submarines and heavy metal doors that can be hermetically sealed.

In Huajiadi, the authorities condemned the underground beneath the building, except for the half basements, which have windows, though they are just as outdated.

"The party chiefs from the district came a week ago and ordered the closing of all the deep basements," the manager of a grocery store explains. "Here, since it's just a half basement, we can go on renting it."

The store owner rents some thirty rooms, but since she has another job during the day, she didn't show up until nightfall.

"We all call her the queen because she's the boss of the basement, and because she's richer than anyone else," a store employee says with some admiration.

"Couldn't you become a queen?" we ask her.

"Never in a million years," she answers, surprised by the depth of our ignorance. "To become the boss of a basement, you have to know someone high up in the party. You need to go through intermediaries, and pay them off. When you get to the top of the pyramid, they're the ones turning over the most cash."

"Our boss is very nice," a resident of the labyrinth chimes in. "Sometimes she makes dumplings with us in the evening, and we even eat together. She rented the whole basement from a guy close to the party, and she sublets it. It's not easy for her. The margins aren't much. She's been renting rooms for more than ten years. We call her the queen, but there's nothing queenly about her."

"The government decided to close down some of the tunnels," explains Lu Huitin, the sociology professor, "but that's not a solution. The government has to assume its responsibilities, protect the rights of this community, and offer social housing at affordable prices. The market economy has led to tremendous rises in rent in Beijing. According to the government, you need at least five square meters [some fifty square feet] for a decent apartment, but that criterion is hardly ever respected. Most rats work in restaurants, or as vendors, watchmen, construction workers, and couriers. Without their contribution, Beijing could not function. It would be paralyzed. The resident permit system is an obstacle for this community as well. It's time to change the rules."

◆

We go to see the manager of a basement in the neighborhood and claim we are interested in renting a room. He tells us he has no worries about being closed down by civil defense.

"Our rooms have passed all the tests and all the examinations the government can throw at them. If you rent from me, you won't have to move again," he promises.

The entrepreneur owns at least 100 rooms, and makes an average of 55,000 yuan (US$7,850) a month, which adds up to 660,000 yuan (about US$95,000) yearly.

"Sometimes a government office will hit us with a sanction and ask us to pay a few thousand yuan, but that's nothing compared to the revenue," he adds, full of self-assurance. "You can make big money in this line of work."

The managers of the underground mostly come from Fujian, a province in the southern reaches of the country whose inhabitants are known for their business sense. Good numbers of kings and queens are also migrants from the provinces of Shandong and Heilongjiang, in the north. Ten years ago, the average annual rent for a basement room in the center of Beijing was only some 30,000 to 40,000 yuan (US$4,300–5,700). After a few small renovations, entrepreneurs could ask for more than 130,000 yuan (US$18,500). At the time, landlords would own at least two or three underground complexes in Beijing and make a veritable fortune. According to a businessman from the city of Zhenghe in Fujian, Beijing can boast as many as 3,000 to 4,000 people from his native town renting out subterranean rooms.

"I'm a peasant and I have no skills, but I can still make my fortune here," he brags to me of his success. "People from Zhenghe represent the biggest community in the business. Solidarity is the key to our success. New arrivals from our region know they can borrow money from us to get into the underground trade. Everybody comes out ahead."

To get authorization to exploit the underground, several people who rent out rooms tell us, you have to not only pay the rent but also bribe people in the municipal services. That way, they know they won't be threatened with a shutdown. Authorization to rent the space goes through several intermediaries before landing with a prospective king. With each pair of hands comes a "transfer payment." At the end of the chain, the underground landlord will have put down an exorbitant sum, impossible without the solidarity of other migrants who have already made it big.

"For a 1,000-square-meter basement [10,760 square feet] in the center of Beijing, the transfer payments can go as high as more than 1 million yuan [US$140,000]," reveals Li Liqiang, who runs a fifteen-room location. "In the government's eyes, the authorization is just a piece of paper. It doesn't suspect it's being resold at such high prices. Still, after three to five years, the transfer payments are amortized. If there weren't those costs, renting out the underground would be a business with exorbitant profits, since the amount of rent paid to civil defense is ridiculous."

But the campaign to close down subterranean lodging in Beijing has moved the Zhenghe businessmen to new, more lucrative horizons.

"Soon, renting out basements will be a dead issue," Li Liqiang decrees. "Now, we're renting fields in exurban regions, near factories and university campuses. The idea is to sign a lease for as long as possible—at least twenty years—and build an apartment building with 100 units. That's more profitable, and more secure."

In the entrails of the Xibahe Zhongli building, a young couple, Haijun and Hongxia, who arrived from Shandong province seven years ago, are managing a basement complex, at least for the time being. Kitschy photos of their wedding, in traditional clothing against a false background, embellish the walls. Wearing the gray slacks and white shirt of an office worker, his hair dyed blond, Haijun describes how he found a job as an employee in a bank, where hopes to move up the ladder. Both young people consider themselves privileged: their 10-square-meter chamber (some 100 square feet), loaded with giant stuffed animals, that they share with their one-year-old, boasts its own window.

Hongxia works as the guard in the basement, which is managed by her father. She receives only a small salary but stays free in exchange for her services.

"Back in the village, everyone told us that real life is living and working in Beijing," she says, smoothing her colorful flowered dress. "It's not just a way to get out of poverty. It's an incredible experience. But I don't know how long we can stand this."

"We're not all kings," Haijun adds, with no shame and a sharp laugh. "My father-in-law is the ruler here. People call us rats, and that sums up the way we live. The kings of the underground reign over the realm of the rats. There's nothing glorious about that."

CHAPTER 11

ARTISTS EMERGING FROM THEIR HOLES

From his days as a rat, he has retained only the fur and the sharp eyes. Cao Yunjin, age thirty-five, with a shaved head, throws a short gray and taupe fur coat over his shoulders as defense against the Beijing winter. Then, as if his subconscious urged him into symbolic metamorphosis, he tosses the fur in his assistant's direction. The young man catches it with one hand in front of a forest of cameras and videos gathered for Cao, who is now revealed in the glory of his midnight-blue satin suit, with a red bow tie and patent-leather shoes. Cao emerged from his rathole more than a dozen years ago, and today he is one of the most popular masters of the *xiangsheng*, a traditional form of comedy routine, known as crosstalk, that is presented as a dialogue between two protagonists, made up of parry and thrust, humorous allusions, imitations, and onomatopoeia, with some singing thrown in. Cao came onto the scene out of nowhere—that is, from Beijing's fetid entrails—to strike it rich. He loves everything that glitters: gold Swiss watches, Italian roadsters in bright hues, femmes fatales—like his second assistant, a willowy Chinese woman with auburn hair, perched on high heels, complete with miniskirt ... I guess she's not afraid of the cold winds.

Cao will sell out Beijing's 1,500-seat Poly Theatre for three straight nights with his one-man show, presented for New Year and revealed to the media as a sneak preview. Front-row seats go for more than 700 yuan (US$100). A backstage pass will set you back more. Cao Yunjin is a phenomenon. He started out as a comedian, and then moved into the movies, becoming a star of the silver screen with a dozen hits to his credit. The Beijing underground hosts a concentration of the human misery of big Chinese cities, but it has also sent up the occasional spark of light. Nothing like the soccer stars who have stepped out of the Brazilian favelas, these successes are so rare that they give no sense of hope to those who live beneath the surface.

Cao Yunjin left his rural hamlet in Hebei province at the age of eighteen and moved to the port city of Tianjin, where he began to study *xiangsheng*. This traditional Chinese art form arose in the country's north. Very much in fashion under the Ming dynasty (1368–1644), this mixture of song and recitation continued to develop in the Qing era (1644–1911). In the People's Republic, it evolved further. Nowadays, it can feature a single artist imitating sounds, or a comic show with several actors. Tianjin has a strong *xiangsheng* tradition, and many well-known artists can be seen in small cabarets there. But Beijing, where the dialect has been imprinted on the art form, is its uncontested capital. Cao moved there in 2001 to study with Guo Degang, an artist famous for his avant-garde approach.

In those days, the bohemian life of young artists, new arrivals to the capital with their dreams of glory, hungry for success—or just plain hungry—was usually limited to a tiny underground room measuring six square meters (around sixty-five square feet) and lit by fluorescents. Cao has very bad memories of that period.

"For five years, I moved all the time, from one basement to the next," he recalls. "Living underground is hard on a person. I was alone. There were no neighbors, no bathroom, no toilet. The spaces weren't as equipped as they are now. The worst place was when a friend lent me his underground art studio. I didn't pay any rent, but the damp was intolerable. I was sick all the time. The worst was what it did to my skin. My chest and back were covered in sores. My arms and feet and hands itched like crazy. I scratched until I bled. I had this obsession: drying my clothes after I washed them. I tried everything, but they wouldn't dry and always smelled like mold. I had to fight for every little thing, every day. But it could have been worse—at least I had a place to stay."

The professional comedian loses his sense of humor when he conjures up his past. He has drawn no inspiration from those days, even if some situations have a certain comic potential.

"I never talk about those things," he declares, disgust in his voice, his eyes dark. "I don't like to. The media are always bringing up my life as a rat. I'd rather forget it. During every TV interview, the journalist will always ask me a question about that, because he thinks it makes a good story. I'm sick of it. And it's even more delicate because the government wants us to talk about positive things. The main thing is to pull yourself out of it. With hard work, it's possible. I'm the proof of that, and I want to give people hope. To lift yourself out of that state, you can't wrap yourself up in dreams. You have to live one day at a time and work hard. Work will lift us out of the hole, not dreams. No sense thinking about the future—the solution is today."

Cao believes the nickname "rat people" is neither insulting nor pejorative.

"It's an expression people use to make fun of themselves, and to help find their inner strength," he says. "Compared to the US and Europe, China is still developing. There are more opportunities for young people today, but it's still a struggle."

When he emerged from the bowels of the city and reached the surface, it was like being reborn. Since those days, he can never get enough light. He has never forgotten that period, for it was crucial to his education.

"When I have problems, I don't take them that seriously," he tells me. "I keep on pushing, moving forward. I'm not afraid of losing what I have, because I know my life has been one enormous stroke of luck."

With the spotlight shining his way, Cao wants to delight in the present, and I am spoiling his moment with questions. He pulls away, and the next minute he has leaped onto the stage, striking a James Bond pose. First on his own, then framed by two shapely ladies. Laying it on thick has become second nature for Cao.

◆

As strange as it sounds, the painter Zhang Siyong, born in 1973, claims he spent the best years of his life in Beijing basements, because that was where he created his body of work. He came to Beijing from Nanchang, in southeastern China, in 1992, and studied design at university. Zhang lived underground for eight years, in the labyrinth beneath Xibahe Zhongli, the upper-class housing development where Shuying, the mother from Shandong, lives these days. But don't tell Zhang that he's part of the rat tribe.

He defines himself as a *bei piao* ("that floats in the north"), a less pejorative term for people who have come to live and work in the large northern cities like Beijing or Tianjin, without ever really settling there because of residency permit problems, people who are still attached to their home province.

An artist, collector, and patron tied to a gallery in the 798 Art Zone, the capital's most prestigious artists' quarter in the Chaoyang neighborhood, Zhang often sells canvases for more than 250,000 yuan (about US$36,000). The exhibition space, with its unique architectural style, is located in the decommissioned buildings of an abandoned military plant and named for the number once used to designate it: 798. The Beijing arts community, which was formed in 1984, started occupying the space in 2000, since the buildings were going for minimal rent. Since those days, after numerous battles to keep the government from closing it down, the 60 hectares (148 acres) of the 798 Art Zone has become an emblematic spot for Beijing culture—and the rents have really taken off.

Zhang's New Millennium Gallery opened in 2002 in hangar 3818 and has been one of the places that count in the contemporary art scene. With his long hair held by a headband, and a white shirt with a skull print, courtesy of an Italian fashion designer, Zhang welcomes us into his cozy, comfortable artist's café, where he often organizes receptions for rich collectors. Seated comfortably in his leather armchair, surrounded by warm woodwork and his art, his success is translated into Cuban cigars and glasses of fine Italian white wine. His most influential figurative and abstract canvases are priced between 2 million and 3 million yuan (US$285,000–430,000).

Zhang asserts that he created his greatest masterpieces—as he calls them—when he lived underground. At the time, he occupied a six-square-meter (sixty-five-square-foot) room below Xibahe

Zhongli and rented an 18-square-meter (nearly 200-square-foot) studio at the same location. He used to leave the studio door open to keep from getting dizzy from the oil paint fumes, which spilled out into the hallway. His canvases didn't dry because of the humidity. With the room lit by fluorescent tubes, he had to retreat into the hallway to get perspective on his paintings.

"The image wasn't stable, I didn't see very well, but I got along," he explains. "I was extremely poor back then. My room didn't have a door, but I had nothing worth stealing. Since there was no natural light, I could wake up at any time of the day or night. It didn't matter. I picked up my brushes and started painting—that's the only thing that counted. I didn't know what the next day would bring. Some days I didn't even know how I would find something to eat. I hardly ever had meat. A lot of the time I was sick, and the solitude was terrible."

Zhang made a living selling small paintings on the street, often for a mouthful of bread. Sometimes he didn't have rent money. When the owner knocked on his door, he wouldn't open it and spent hours crouching on the floor to avoid being spotted. Some months, he managed to convince an old neighbor lady to lend him the 200 yuan (US$30). She agreed because, like him, she came from Jiangxi province. The world of human rats is one of extreme individualism, and help comes only from people from the same village or province.

"Before, my money troubles ran in the hundreds of yuan. Now, they're in the millions. But I'm tougher, thanks to the experience of living underground. The ordeal contributed to my success. I was in love with a woman, but I gave myself entirely to my art. I had no office hours. I painted day and night. Sometimes I went out to see a rock concert, then I climbed back down into my hole. I've continued to paint, but no canvas has succeeded in reaching the level of what I did back then. I lived as a recluse. When I went up to live on the surface in 2001, I discovered the world, and social life. I met my wife and I had a son."

Zhang's works were not directly inspired by his experiences underground. Instead, painting was his means of escape. A way of leaving behind his daily life in the dark, half-lit universe. He imagined a world exploding with color that reflected his inner feelings, his lust for life and light, his need for love. Some of his abstract paintings are allegories of his existence, and refer back to the transformation of his village of Nanchang by urbanization. He accepts the influence of Monet and the pointillists, and lets his imagination wander, using their techniques with more modern themes or in nonfigurative canvases. Since he never went to art school, he discovered the great artists of the past in books. His early works were homages to them. In China, an homage is often understood as nothing else but copying someone, but not in Zhang's case: he was able to adapt their techniques and make them his own. His parents were peasants, but he couldn't picture spending his life in the fields, living in poverty, while the country was developing all around him. So he decided to try his luck in Beijing.

"My father died when I was young," he relates, as if this setback were a stroke of luck that pushed him to seek a greater destiny, instead of remaining stuck with a lesser model. Although he feels a deep separation from the world of his parents, Zhang is proud of his origins.

"My mother never understood my work. She thought I was painting portraits in the street and showing my work on the sidewalk. Once I invited her to an opening. She didn't say a word, but she never stopped smiling. My origins have had a great influence on me. Especially Nanchang. They used to say it was the Venice of China. In my work, there is always water, the seasons, rivers, and flowers."

Zhang's life changed in 1998, when a big hotel in the Sanlitun district offered him the chance to show his paintings over a twenty-day period. At the end of the show, as he was about to wrap everything up, an American businessman appeared. He bought forty of the sixty-eight paintings on display. In one fell swoop, Zhang earned 250,000 yuan (about US$36,000), more than he'd ever had in his whole life.

"It was a real fortune back then," Zhang remembers. "I invited all my friends down to my basement. The poorest of the poor had the chance to taste the finest drinks. The morning after, I woke up alone, surrounded by empty bottles, posters from my show scattered all over. I was happy. I like thinking back to those years. Though I couldn't live like that again."

Lady Luck continued to smile upon him that year with the opening of Beijing's first French restaurant, called Flo, where he showed his works. The foreign patrons were introduced to his work, and a few months later, he was chosen to exhibit his paintings for ten days at the National Art Museum of China, which opened the doors to fame. In 1999, he signed a five-year contract with a Hong Kong agent for the sale of twenty works a year at 10,000 yuan (about US$1,500) each. He used the money to open his first gallery. He was only twenty-five. The gallery was located in an underground hallway next to a McDonald's. He showed the work of other young artists there, as his way of giving them a chance.

"None of them ever really made it," he says regretfully but without much conviction. "Those artists who came to Beijing had one thing in mind, and that was to adapt to what the market wanted. Some of them were talented, but their work had no soul. I expressed my true feelings in my art, and I didn't care about the market."

◆

I was pretty proud to have uncovered this treasure: a famous painter who had emerged from the underground. I mentioned Zhang to an artist friend who has been living in Beijing for a number of years.

"Right, New Millennium!" my friend exclaimed. "That guy is a bastard. I didn't know anything about his background, but I can tell you he's a real rat."

Zhang had waxed enthusiastic about my friend's work and offered to put on a show of his paintings in his gallery. The canvases were chosen and the opening set, but a few weeks before, Zhang disappeared. He stopped answering the phone, and his gallery announced he had traveled to the countryside for an urgent matter.

"Typical Chinese," my friend lamented (he happens to be married to a woman from Beijing). "He didn't want to admit that he'd found something else to show that would sell better. So he disappeared into thin air until I understood that he'd tricked me like a fool."

I should have sniffed out Zhang's blind ambition when he proudly showed me his photo collection on his smartphone: pictures of him with former French president Jacques Chirac, the actors Sophie Marceau and Christopher Lambert, and Nobel laureates who had bought his paintings. His prize photo showed a Chinese billionaire giving one of his canvases to former vice president Al Gore. I fell for the carefully crafted story of how he rose to fame, and how he tried to carry his friends up with him.

"Steve Jobs collected my paintings," he swore, "but I don't have a photo. My family's history is 500 years old. I am the first painter ever. My dream is to be shown in Europe."

Zhang respects the codes of political conduct, spoken and unspoken. In private, he won't beat around the bush when it comes to expressing his hard feelings for the current regime. But in public, when faced with a foreigner, he will immediately launch into President Xi Jinping's dialectic reasoning, and his dreams of renewal and grandeur for the People's Republic. With its all-seeing eye, the state knows what the intelligentsia thinks, and it tolerates criticism—as long as it is expressed discreetly, in private, and doesn't lean toward agitation or rebellion. A quick study, Zhang even supports Xi's initiative to send peasants to the country to be "reeducated." The regime imposes strict censorship on all public figures suspected of questioning its authority, such as internationally known artist Ai Weiwei. At the same time, however, the easing of control over the domestic art market, most notably in the visual arts, has led to the development of spectacular artistic creation over the last twenty years or so. The Communist "rectification" campaign as it is applied to artists is meant to help them "acquire the correct point of view regarding art" by having contact with the "rural masses," according to Xi. That initiative seems to have sprung fully formed from the Maoist period, when the regime's founder sent millions of Chinese intellectuals to the countryside to be "reeducated" by the peasants. Xi has denounced the "vulgarity" of some artwork, urging creators to promote "socialist values," patriotism, and "serving the people," leading the official press to compare him to Mao. By "living among the masses," the "workers of art and literature" will "be stimulated in the acquisition of a correct point of view about art and create more masterpieces," according to the document that puts forward this initiative, which was quoted by the official state-run news agency, *New China*.

Zhang is very proud to have been chosen by the Central Party School of the Communist Party in 2014 to be part of a seminar and happily exhibits his hammer and sickle insignia. Not that he has been seduced by its dusty ideological veneer, but the networks offered by the party are a powerful path to success in the People's Republic. Though his support does have its limits: he does not intend to go get reeducated among the masses.

"I come from the countryside, and I've never broken ties with it," he claims with overstated sincerity. "Xi's request concerns official artists whom the government pays a fixed salary, giving them a stable income. For them, it is essential to be reeducated among the peasants. There are 500 million of them. They need art produced for them. We can't ignore them and make art only for city people."

Carried upward by his success, the artist has little regard for his former tribe. "Of course there is poverty among the rat people," he admits, "but they're not sleeping in the streets. It's not that bad. Besides, for a lot of them, it's temporary. No one made them come to Beijing and live underground. It was their choice. In America and Europe, you have welfare for the poor, and that's good. But it's impossible in China because there are just too many people."

The enormous challenges caused by a population of an estimated 1.4 billion individuals, whom the country is working to move progressively into the modern age, are very real. Yet the size of the population is also an excuse the party uses to justify a multitude of mistakes and missteps—starting with the absence of democracy and a strict social framework that offers no room for what we consider basic freedoms. Obsessed with its own survival, the Chinese Communist Party promotes its version of the indispensable "harmony," arguing that "Western values" would weaken the country and cast it irremediably into chaos.

◆

The success of Zhang Xi, a young actor, is still precarious. He served three years in subterranean Beijing before working his way to the surface, up to the light, in the spring of 2015. During his first months in the city, he rented a 4-square-meter (45 square-foot) room for 300 yuan (US$40) a month, then moved on to 8 square meters (85 square feet) for twice the price, before graduating to a 20-square-meter (215-square-foot) suite—a luxury that set him back 1,000 yuan (US$140) a month. Today he lives in a one-room place, 15 square meters (160 square feet), its walls covered in photos of Marlon Brando, Woody Allen, and Mia Farrow, in a run-down building on the outskirts of the city. Living in daylight costs him 2,000 yuan (US$285) a month, a fortune considering his small income.

"In my student days, I couldn't afford anything better," he recalls. "And I didn't want to ask my parents for money. My conditions were pretty bad. I had to line up for the shower. My room was always damp and I only stayed there a few hours a night to sleep. The rest of the time I went out. It was the only way not to get sick. I was constantly concerned about safety. If there had been a fire, as often happens underground, no one in the labyrinth where over 100 people lived would have survived. There was no ventilation. You couldn't breathe. You have to stop thinking about it. Otherwise, you get suicidal."

His father visited him once. When he saw the state in which his son was living, he insisted on paying for a place above ground, but Zhang Xi would not accept.

"Even if you eat poison every day, you're still alive," he says with a laugh. "You wake up every morning and it's the same miracle: you're alive. For my generation, it's normal to live below ground for a while. One day, an old man told me it was a shame that my parents let me live like that—in a hole. That opened my eyes. I wasn't competent enough to live decently. I had to make an effort to get a better life. Today, I'm making more and more money, and that's why I decided to migrate to the surface. To be a man, you have to improve your situation, little by little."

Zhang Xi originally came from Inner Mongolia, where his parents settled in the 1990s and opened a restaurant. He studied theater at university in X'ian, the former imperial capital, in Shanxi province. He found a stable job there as an actor in the municipal theater for 2,000 yuan (US$285) a month. In the end, he traveled to Beijing in search of a better fortune. With his cereal-bowl haircut and his off-white tunic over a pair of green pants, Zhang Xi cultivates a wise artist look. His parts in small plays mean he makes enough to eat and drink with his friends. To pay the rent and have some pocket money, he turns into an itinerant street vendor selling stone necklaces.

"Beijing people look down on us who've come here from the provinces to work," he says, letting go a bitter puff of cigarette smoke. "With rats, it's even worse. People on the surface don't know anything about our lives. That's why they're afraid of us. Some of them throw their garbage into our basements. In my place, there were all kinds of people: merchants who made tens of thousands of yuan a month but preferred to save on rent, sex workers, students, waiters, cooks. Some people here who have an apartment would rather rent it out and live underground. With the way rents are going up, they can make a lot of money doing that."

Zhang Xi has his own dream. He wants a career in the movies, and enough money to support his parents, his future wife, and his children.

CHAPTER 12

THE BILLIONAIRES AND THE RATS

Only a few floors separate the sunlit world from the shadowy hallways inhabited by the rat tribe, but sometimes it seems like the distance can be measured in light-years. Like on Friday and Saturday evenings, at the Workers' Stadium in the Chaoyang district. Every weekend, the same ritual: Beijing's young jet set engages in its favorite pastime, letting their V8 and V12 engines roar from beneath the hoods of their Italian muscle cars, goosing the accelerator as they search for a parking spot around the stadium. The masters of these beasts all display the same self-satisfied, impassive look.

Built in 1959, to celebrate the tenth anniversary of the creation of the People's Republic, the Workers' Stadium was one of the key locations of the Cultural Revolution. "Revisionists" and other "reactionaries" were forced to confess to their crimes

—real or imaginary—humiliated and beaten there in front of enormous crowds of spectators. Today, surrounded with bars and nightclubs, the stadium has become one of the hot spots of Beijing nightlife that play host to the Red princes, the spoiled-rotten heirs to the revolution, who have converted to runaway capitalism, the wheels of their Ferraris as red as the Chinese flag, with a few neon apple-green Lamborghinis and pretty pink Maseratis thrown in.

The main attraction for the party's children is the Fugu Luxurious American Club, the place to play for those who enjoy conspicuous consumption, especially when it comes to cars. These Beijing show-offs also have a taste for the high-end British companies like Bentley and Rolls-Royce. The clientele sinks deep into leather sofas, surrounded by woodwork reminiscent of an English club, though shiny opulence and kitschy taste are more the rule. Conversations among friends are broken by long silences as they stare at their smartphone screens. Young women shoot serial selfies in front of the collector cars or against the backdrop of a crystal wall.

The Red princes favor enormous private salons, illuminated by Baccarat chandeliers and equipped with giant screens and individual sound systems. They go crazy for karaoke, switching between languid love songs in an adolescent tremolo, accompanied by pretty and very sophisticated chanteuses, and more rhythmic selections in English, a language they reproduce with approximate phonetics. The whole shebang is washed down by Dom Pérignon champagne, Hennessy XO cognac, and Moutai, the premium Chinese liqueur enjoyed by the elite. Every bottle is presented to the foreign guest with the guarantee that the finest beverages have been carefully chosen for him ahead of time. Three glasses, carefully filled with each of the three drinks, are served. A series of *ganbei* begins, wherein one must drink to friendship.

This poisonous combination quickly produces a head-spinning effect and destroys any will to communicate in coherent fashion. Enormous trays of exotic fruit, served on a platform of dry ice for that smoky atmosphere, are supposed to sponge up the alcohol. My multiple attempts to take my leave have all been aborted, interrupted by endless group selfie sessions, followed by another deadly round of drinks. After several hours of this torture, a sudden ray of lucidity has me running for the door.

◆

The owner of the Fugu bar, Lu Gao, a thirty-two-year-old billionaire, made his fortune in used luxury cars. His activities helped him forge solid links with the rich heirs of party leaders, and find the backing he needed to diversify his investments. At the end of the afternoon, he pulls up to the bar at the wheel of a white Maserati, accompanied by two female assistants driving impressive Cadillacs. His head shaved, wearing a skin-tight white T-shirt and baggy black shorts and Vans sneakers, Lu Gao looks more like a skateboarder than a shrewd businessman. His Number One assistant, a tall, elegant young woman, introduces herself in English, offering a limp hand. Her fingernails are decorated with gold polish and sparkles that match her latest-model iPhone. From her two Louis Vuitton handbags, one set inside the other, she produces the newest ultra-slim MacBook and sets it on her knees. Number Two assistant does the same. They take scrupulous notes on everything their boss says in every meeting, but first, Number One offers this hilarious explanation.

"Please excuse the boss, he just got out of a very long meeting. He went to take a piss, but he won't be long. Our schedule is absolutely hellish. We have meetings until three or four in the morning almost every night. The bar is good for business."

I do my best to stifle an attack of the giggles. The scene with the assistant reminds me of a weekend I spent with my wife in a provincial city in the heart of the country. We touched down in an unlikely five-star hotel fitted out with modern decor. As the receptionist, who had obviously been chosen for her sophisticated demeanor, was entering our passport information into her computer, she broke off and slipped down behind the counter. She proceeded to hawk up a rich gob, then stood up, and spat noisily into the wastebasket. I was astonished and didn't dare look at Laetitia, but it was no use—we both exploded in a combination of laughter and embarrassment. Everywhere you go in China, except perhaps in the most remote regions, you are struck by the great progress after thirty years of development, rapid modernization, and the will to join the trends of globalization. But when some small sign betrays just how fast this progress has gone, such as when a waiter tries to open a bottle of champagne with a corkscrew, you can't help but smile at the contrast.

Obsessed with the material pleasures that their instant fortune has delivered, some ultrarich Chinese people have not had time to acquire the etiquette and polite manners of high society. Lu Gao belongs to that group. Stretched out on a vast leather sofa, his speech is broken by a mishmash of sniffles and coughing. His small black eyes sparkle with intelligence from the chubby folds of his baby face. Born in 1983, Gao left university after six months, in 2000, and went into business. In 2002, he sold his first bar, which he had opened in Beijing to launch his empire with an initial investment of some US$11,250. Today, he stands atop a fortune estimated at US$1.7 billion, with shares in automobiles, real estate, high-tech research, and jewelry. The Fugu bar in Beijing, a temple of collector cars, is his latest showpiece. And it won't be his last. Gao has plans to open one in every major city in the country and—why not?—in Paris, too.

He is convinced that his bars will be to cars what the Hard Rock Cafe is to electric guitars. The jewel in his crown is a shiny black 1937 Rolls-Royce, which is on display in the center of the bar and worth some US$9.2 million. Next to it stand a Cobra, and another Rolls, which belonged to Cary Grant. Among Gao's sixty or so luxury vehicles, parked neatly in a garage, there are a number of treasures, such as Audrey Hepburn's Ferrari, a Bentley that belonged to Madonna, and a Rolls that used to be Dustin Hoffman's.

"It's a good investment," he points out, stroking the 1937 Rolls. "Take this one. Its value goes up seventeen percent a year. For some people, dropping out of school is a disaster. For me, university was a waste of time. Businesses were being created and I wanted to be part of that. At the time, you could still find unexploited sectors, virgin lands that could be farmed, and without competition. That's what I did with used luxury cars. For people getting started now, competition is a lot tougher. There is plenty of talent on the market these days, which is why you can't get anywhere in this country without a solid network. I was lucky. I caught the last high-speed train to success."

Gao belongs to a club with an increasing membership. Numbers fluctuate and are sometimes contradictory, and fortunes rise and fall, but as of 2018, Beijing had outstripped New York for the highest number of billionaires: 131 and counting, as opposed to 92 for the Big Apple. China is home to the most billionaires in the world at 819, outdoing the United States at 571, and is gaining new ones at the fastest rate—210 that year. The average fortune of the thousand richest Chinese people stands at $1.4 billion, according to the latest changing figures. Real estate is their main source of wealth, despite the government's attempts to limit acquisitions and stabilize prices. In 2016, the number of ultrarich individuals with a personal fortune of at least 100 million yuan (US$14.3 million) reached 89,000. That year, Guangdong, a southern province, replaced Beijing in boasting the highest number of people with at least 10 million yuan (US$1.4 million) in assets. According to Bloomberg, China is expected to turn out millionaires three times as fast as the US. The country's total wealth has risen 1,300 percent over the course of the twenty-first century.

After he took over the Communist Party in 2012, President Xi Jinping launched an austerity program and an anti-corruption campaign that battered the luxury product market. On the one hand, the ultrarich, who owe their fortune to links with party higher-ups, were forced to be discreet, but they continued getting richer. On the other hand, the outrageous social inequalities in China lessened only marginally in recent years. They remain egregious, fed by the gap between the urban and rural populations, according to official figures published in January 2014. China's Gini coefficient, which is a measure of equality in a country's distribution of wealth, stood at 0.468 in 2018, which is a cause for concern, as it ranked among the least equal nations. "According to international criteria, a coefficient higher than 0.4 means there are major inequalities when it comes to sharing wealth," says Ma Jiantang, the director of the National Bureau of Statistics. Ma reveals that the average income of the urban population is 3.03 times higher than in rural areas, even if the latter have undergone a faster progression. The disparities in the world's second-largest economy are a source of discontent among the population. According to a recent Peking University study, one percent of the richest households in China control more than one-third of the country's wealth; whereas twenty-five percent of the poorest households possess scarcely one percent of China's wealth. World Bank figures reveal that, in 2014, some 200 million Chinese lived below the poverty line, on less than US$1.25 a day. The party is trying to reduce inequality, and contain the risk of an explosion of discontent that could be fatal to it. But there is still a long way to go.

"In 2008, when the Olympics were on, the local authorities wanted to expel the rats," explains Hu Xingdou, economics professor at the Beijing Institute of Technology. "They soon saw that was impossible. There wouldn't have been anyone left to sweep the streets, sell the vegetables, or build buildings. Beijing would have been paralyzed without them. In a city, all levels of society have to coexist harmoniously. But in China, working conditions are not normal, the distribution of wealth is not reasonable, and there are no real unions. To climb the social ladder requires a struggle every step of the way, so rigid is the class system. The upper classes enjoy privileges that seem to be cast in stone. The *hukou* system prevents migrants from changing their lives. The *mingong* are forced to renounce their peasant identity when they go to work in the big cities but without enjoying the rights of city dwellers, such as a social safety net. The government imposes strict limits on their rights in an effort to regulate urbanization by pushing them to settle in small and midsize cities, but there aren't enough jobs for them there.

"Sooner or later, the government is going to have to do something. In a country where economic development is the priority, efficiency is important. But we can't ignore inequalities. The state must institute a minimum wage to guarantee employees' income. Unions must be created to protect their rights. Strikes must be made legal to force businesses to give in to certain demands. Charitable associations need to be allowed. In China, only official organizations have the right to undertake humanitarian activities. There are very few NGOs, which should be playing an important role in improving the living conditions of the poor."

For billionaire Lu Gao, inequalities are a "necessary evil" in a developing country like China. At the same time, he recognizes the "significant" contribution of the rat people at the bottom of the social ladder, when it comes to building the cities of the new empire.

"The rats are indispensable when it comes to our cities," he states. "They are like the plodding yellow oxen that labor without ceasing. Without them, Beijing would be a desert. They do all the dirty jobs—build the city, drive those little delivery rickshaws. All that for pennies. There are three categories: Those who accept the dirty jobs but have ambitions for something greater. Those who have no dreams and want only to survive. They will never get anywhere. And those who contribute to society without asking for anything in return. They are the rarest kind."

His judgment is without cynicism but also without the slightest compassion, and with all the brutality of which the new Chinese capitalists are capable.

Gao believes that some members of the rat tribe will succeed, even spectacularly so. "It takes a lot of courage," he says with some admiration. "In Mao's China, people were lazy. It was simple: they had no ambition to own a Ferrari or a Lamborghini, or succeed in any other way. Now they are driven by that motor that pushes them to strive for the top. Luckily, Communism isn't possible in today's China."

His honesty shocks me. "What about the Chinese Communist Party?" I exclaim. "What good is it if Communism isn't possible?"

Gao tries to cover his tracks. "China is a socialist country," he declares.

◆

Within the rat tribe, women have their model for success. Zhou Qunfei did not emerge from their ranks, though she does come from the bottom level, very close to theirs. Born in 1970, Zhou was once a worker in a factory that made screens for cell phones. After learning about the industry, in 2003, she launched her own company that now provides touch screens for Apple, Samsung, and other tech giants. In 2018, her fortune as CEO of Lens Technology reached US$19.8 billion, making her one of the richest women in China, and the world's richest self-made woman. Zhou maintains an eighty-nine-percent share in her company, and her screens are used on one smartphone in five around the world.

But she has stayed humble. "I believe it's important not to get too giddy when you have success, and not fall apart when times are tough," she has said.

Zhou was born to a poor family in Hunan province. Her father was blinded after an accident in the 1960s, and her mother died when she was five. She left school at fifteen. Her detractors, essentially men, accuse her of having built her fortune by marrying the owner of her screen factory. After her divorce, she went on to launch a competing firm.

By contrast, Lu Gao has never had any trouble making ends meet. He comes from the Red middle class: his father was a factory director, and his mother worked as an insurance broker. Yet he claims he has done his part to help reduce social inequalities— notably in his companies, which have 1,000 employees in China, including 300 temporary workers.

"Of course, we do have employees who make modest amounts of money," he admits, unembarrassed. "But none of them lives underground, as far as I know. We provide meals and lodging to our maintenance people, who make the lowest salaries. And we do a lot of charitable work. We spend more than 4 million yuan [US$570,000] a year: Thirty percent for victims of natural catastrophes, such as fires, floods, and earthquakes. Then twenty percent for children who have been left behind so they can go to school, and fifty percent for initiatives that increase the company's visibility. Party bureaucrats who have gotten rich in unsavory ways do charitable work to try and improve their image and extend their network."

But that's not him, Gao swears, as serious as can be. He has the privilege of choosing every morning between his Porsche, his Maserati, his Lamborghini, and his Rolls, complete with chauffeur, to travel to his office—thanks to his own hard work.

"Family and social responsibilities have developed at the same time as success," he tells me earnestly, though I can't be sure how sincere he really is. "There is no success without social responsibility. I have a good heart, I love society, and I want to give back some of what I have earned."

Yet the last years have not been easy for Gao, who has had to deal with the effects of President Xi Jinping's anti-corruption campaign. With this operation to clean up rival factions, or those within the party who challenge his supreme authority, there are now fewer Red princes who would dare buy a used Ferrari or Lamborghini. The toys that the party's children love to play with have become a little too ostentatious for the higher-ups, who are worried about the millions of citizens who wonder online how those kids can afford Italian roadsters on a monthly salary that's supposed to top out at US$1,700. Sports car accidents can be deadlier for the parents of the young merrymakers than for the young drivers themselves. Acts of corruption are punishable by death.

In the spring of 2015, a Lamborghini and a Ferrari slammed into one another in Beijing in a road race in a tunnel with other similar vehicles. The fact that the most recent *Fast and the Furious* movie had just hit the screens might have had something to do with it. The neighbors were exasperated by races organized in the tunnel near the Bird's Nest, the distinctive Olympic stadium.

Photos of the green Lamborghini, the red Ferrari, and several other banged-up but unidentifiable cars were extremely popular online after the accident, which injured one person. According to the Sina Corp site, which quoted police sources, at least one of the drivers was a student. The police were roundly mocked online because of their version of the event, which described the cars as "small passenger vehicles."

Lamborghinis are sold in China for around US$865,000, and Ferraris go for $540,000.

"Who were the drivers? And who are their families?" commenters on Weibo wanted to know. Rumors discussing the "Red pedigree" of these young speed demons were quickly deleted from the net.

An earlier Ferrari accident in March 2012 in Beijing set off a political seismic shift. The driver, who was killed on the spot, turned out to be the son of Ling Jihua, former Chinese president Hu Jintao's right-hand man. Two young women were found in the wreckage, seriously injured, and one was naked. Ferrari set off a storm of online derision with its press release claiming it did not understand how this could happen, since the vehicle involved "was strictly a two-seater." The incident inflamed the debate about corruption in high places and the behavior of Chinese leaders. Ling Jihua was fired and charged with corruption.

Lu Gao isn't worried about Red princes being involved in spectacular car accidents. They aren't bad for business—quite the contrary.

"The first thing they think about after they climb out of the wreck is the next model they're going to buy," he says, laughing. "A few days later, I get a call. Normally, they're very proud of themselves when the papers relate their exploits. They figure they're superheroes. There's competition among them for who can have the most spectacular accident."

Crouching in the city's entrails, the rat tribe observes the spectacle with strange fascination, and without any feeling that they are witnessing the twilight of an empire.

"The Western countries have their royal families," says Wang Xiuqing, who lived in a sewer for ten years. "We have our Red princes."

CHAPTER 13

THE ALL-POWERFUL PARTY: GOD OF THE RATS

Total failure. That was the result of my attempts to meet municipal officials, either from the government or the Communist Party, and question them about the fate of the rat people.

That was to be expected, but all the same, an administration that brought 400 million people out of poverty must have something to say for itself. And, in theory, a Communist Party leader with the will to open up the country to the rest of the world should take advantage of every opportunity to advertise his efforts to raise up the laboring masses and reduce society's inequalities. The social fiber is not the regime's strong point, however, and the requests I sent to various departments went unanswered.

A few months after I arrived in China, I had a most edifying meeting with Wu Jianmin. He was a diplomat, ambassador, and former spokesman for the Ministry of Foreign Affairs of the

People's Republic of China, who died in 2016. He also worked to have Shanghai named host of Expo 2010.

"When I was ambassador to France, the government there had just brought in the thirty-five-hour workweek," he told me. "When I described that to Chinese leaders, they started laughing and couldn't stop. 'France? It's bringing in measures to destroy its ability to compete. Work creates wealth. With a thirty-five-hour workweek, it has created a welfare mentality that encourages laziness.' That's what made the Chinese leaders laugh."

The Chinese Communist Party was fascinated by the success of the United States, and it took what might be useful for it, to help put the country on the road to quick development—without ever considering the idea of equal opportunity for all, or the American democratic system. At the beginning of the economic opening kicked off by Deng Xiaoping, at the end of the 1970s, China could not afford the luxury of a social safety net. Since then, it has never been a priority, as nothing was allowed to slow down the competitiveness of the world's factory. The party called its model "socialism with Chinese characteristics," and the country progressively converted to the market economy, without ever completing a changeover to more liberal values. In the space of a few years, the party brass all became nineteenth-century capitalists —the kind before antitrust laws came in to regulate business operations and protect consumers from predatory companies through fair competition. As a result, Communist leaders divvied up entire sectors of the country's economy into state monopolies, or state-owned enterprises (SOEs). As China experienced phenomenal growth, the families of those leaders built colossal fortunes within these enterprises, or by running companies that signed juicy contracts with them. Then the Red princes, the heirs of the first-generation economic managers, turned out to be copies of the Great Gatsby, Chinese-style. Corruption became a generalized fact, making the entire system rotten. And the rat tribe continued to be seen as cheap labor, indispensable fuel for the system that made them rich.

Meanwhile, the Communist Party became obsessed with its survival as the head of the state. Since there are no democratic elections in China, the party is bound to the people through a tacit pact guaranteeing them growing prosperity—the modern version of the Mandate of Heaven by which the emperors reigned over this country as vast as a continent ... until they were overthrown by a new dynasty. So despite slowing growth, salaries continue to rise and more than 10 million jobs are created each year. Still, the pact between the party and the people has become fragile. In such conditions, further economic slowdown is a threat. All the more so since the people are sick of the party members' thievery.

"If prices rise massively and people lose their jobs, social agitation and political revolt are possible," says economics professor Hu Xingdou. "But I don't see an economic crisis hitting China. More like a gradual slowing of growth."

The economic model of the People's Republic has run out of steam in recent years. As salaries increased, the country became less competitive than other Southeast Asian countries that produce for less. It can no longer claim to be the world's factory and must change its scale, and turn into the creative center of the world. Severe social inequality, the lack of a safety net, the extreme pollution caused by unchecked development, and an overall feeling of insecurity are serious challenges. But to change the system and liberate creative energies, power has no choice— it must break up the state monopolies that absorb nearly all investment. But then it would challenge the financial interests of powerful factions within the party.

With its 1.4 billion people, China harbors a gigantic under-exploited market, but experts wonder about the Communist authorities' ability to make the necessary changes. The country aims to retool its economic model by turning to high-tech industries, consumer goods, and services. But starting in the summer of 2015, the economic slowdown caused a swell of concern that led to panicked selling on the stock markets. The successive devaluations of the yuan shook the world economy. Rich Chinese bought fewer French luxury goods and fewer German sedans, and spent less on overseas travel, since the cost of those goods and services rose with a weaker yuan.

But the biggest effect for the Chinese was the bursting of the stock market bubble of 2015. The markets had risen in value by 150 percent in just one year. People with small amounts of savings put all their money into stocks, retirees poured their pensions into the market, and some even went into debt to invest in local shares that seemed to offer unlimited growth. Then the Shanghai Stock Exchange lost more than 40 percent in three months. Some small investors suffered big losses. Just barely making ends meet, very few of the rat tribe have anything left over for stocks, but everyone was affected by the economic slowdown and volatile markets.

Even the captains of industry suffered, and hesitated to invest more in their country. For many years China's number one tycoon (he has been replaced by Ma Huateng, at least for now), Wang Jianlin, president and founder of the Wanda Group that specializes in real estate and entertainment, lost US$3.6 billion, or ten percent of his value, in one single day at the end of August 2015. Before the tumult, in 2013, Wang Jianlin welcomed me into his office overlooking all of Beijing, in his imposing glass tower in the CBD. The occasion: a cup of tea and some comments about the Chinese economy. His father was a hero of the People's Liberation Army, a comrade-in-arms of Mao, and he himself is a former army officer, ex-bureaucrat, and party member in the roiling port city of Dalian. Close to the party brass, he had the greatest *guanxi* of all businessmen at the time, though the wheel of fortune has turned since then. He has had to sell off notable assets to repay debts, but in his glory days, he had the state smiling upon him by investing in sectors where China wants to display its soft power, such as entertainment and soccer teams. Yet he also knew how to speak truth to power—he advised leaders to stop their policy of artificially stimulating growth, to which they were addicted, and settle for a solid, measured rate of four percent to five percent.

"China has no choice but to liberalize, since it is now part of the global system," he told me. His hair carefully parted, his suit impeccable, he spoke serenely, though he no doubt felt the storm gathering. "The state cannot go on running the economy in a closed system. We must push the government to liberate the energies of private enterprise on every level. My greatest wish is to put an end to the system of monopolies and for all sectors to be accessible to private enterprise. State-run businesses and the private sector must occupy a level playing field."

Ever faithful to the party, Wang Jianlin displays his trust in Xi Jinping but is less enthusiastic about the return to Maoist values recommended by the new Red emperor.

"The dictatorship of the proletariat and permanent revolution preached by Mao Zedong no longer correspond to our era," he declares, sipping his green tea. "Under Mao, the Chinese economy was in ruins. We had lots of catching up to do in every area. From the Communist Revolution and the disaster of the Cultural Revolution, we should retain one lesson that the party in power must heed—it must never lose sight of economic development and the aspirations of the people."

◆

Since he took power at the end of 2012, President Xi Jinping has tightened his control over the party and the country. Xi believes that abuse of power made the Soviet system collapse from within, and he thinks his party must prepare for the same danger. He launched a full-scale anti-corruption campaign, promising to destroy the "tigers"—the top party leaders—as well as the "flies"—small-time scheming bureaucrats. His campaign to clean house is quite popular. Month after month, announcements are made of investigations and firings: from state consortiums to the former Minister of Public Security Zhou Yongkang to high-ranking military officers, including the former vice president of the party's powerful Central Military Commission. No one seems safe. Xi's campaign against corrupt officials has caused much nervousness and embarrassment among party ranks. He has turned it into an imposing weapon to eliminate his adversaries and concentrate power in his own hands, in the process becoming the country's most powerful leader since Mao. Yet many doubt his actual efficiency. For political scientist Zhang Lifan, "his anti-corruption campaign has caused stagnation of the state machine and divisions within the party."

The new Red emperor reigns over the People's Republic with an iron fist and a smooth smile. Xi's method is tried and true. He resurrected hard-and-fast Marxist ideology, subscribes to old-school Maoism, and will not suffer the slightest protest, which is repressed without a second thought. His popularity is high among the common people, especially the rat tribe, who see in him a version of Mr. Clean. Thanks to the censorship of online sources in China, he has been spared rumors of profiteering by his family.

Xi Jinping dusted off party ideology by trying to build a bridge between Mao and Deng Xiaoping, the father of reform, while correcting the excesses. His strategy of the Four Comprehensives aimed to build a "moderately prosperous society," "deepen reform," "govern the nation according to law," and "strictly govern the Party." But the Marxist veneer is tinted with Confucian values and a nationalism that some consider dangerous, since it can potentially escape his control.

"Some elements do play in his favor," says Jean-Pierre Cabestan, a professor of political science at Hong Kong Baptist University. "China needs social protection and redistribution. Xi wants to show that he can guarantee welfare and justice, and that he has inclusive policies that will bring harmony to society. In reality, he is on the side of business. His problem is that no one really believes in his ideology."

The country's press is strictly controlled by Communist authorities who have imprisoned dozens of journalists, lawyers, university professors, and ordinary internet users, muzzling dissident voices in an unprecedented censorship effort not seen for years. The People's Republic has chosen to strictly limit the work of foreign NGOs. Morale is low among associations in China that fight for workers' rights, against discrimination, or for progress in health and education. The living conditions and lives of the bottom dogs are not going to get better anytime soon. The party has decided to see NGOs as a security risk, not a partner.

"Protest and the development of civil society are generally not tolerated," says Joseph Chen, an expert in Chinese politics at the City University of Hong Kong.

"All internal studies of Chinese power point to protests increasing in the years to come," predicts Nicholas Bequelin, Amnesty International's regional director for East and Southeast Asia. "The party is preparing for this by taking tactical measures to try and limit the risk. It is preventing civil society from creating institutions, thereby keeping it from becoming a force. If they are defending workers' rights or gender equality, NGOs can be tolerated for a few years, but if they build up too much influence or become an embarrassment, they will be wiped out."

The government represses anyone who, in their eyes, presents a potential threat. The party has become an expert at silencing the internet, which, at one point, had become a public forum for critics of the regime. An army of censors was sent into action. Web hosts who are not ideologically zealous enough can be shut down. In September 2011, the Supreme People's Court announced penalties of three years in prison for anyone disseminating "libelous" information shared more than 500 times or seen more than 5,000 times online.

When he took power, Xi called upon the party to learn "profound lessons" from the fall of the Soviet Union. "Why did the Soviet Union disintegrate? Why did the Soviet Communist Party fall apart? An important reason is that their ideals and convictions had weakened," he said in a speech given to party members in 2012. "In the end, all it took was one word from Gorbachev to declare the dissolution of the Soviet CP. And when it happened, not a single man had the courage to stand up and resist."

Whereas Xi decided to take control, with an iron fist, of the Chinese CP and the country ... at the risk of accelerating the end of the Communist regime.

This is the idea proposed by David Shambaugh, a well-known American expert on China, which had all the impact of a bomb in Beijing. Shambaugh is a political science professor at George Washington University, and in 2015, researchers at the China Foreign Affairs University, which works very closely with the party in power, named him the second most influential China expert in the United States.

Until then, Shambaugh was known for his benevolent attitude toward the regime. But then in a *Wall Street Journal* article titled "The Coming Chinese Crackup," he wrote, "In spite of appearances, China's political system is badly broken and nobody knows it better than the Communist Party itself. China's strongman leader, Xi Jinping, is hoping that a crackdown on dissent and corruption will shore up the party's rule. He is determined to avoid becoming the Mikhail Gorbachev of China, presiding over the party's collapse ... His despotism is severely stressing China's system and society—and bringing it closer to a breaking point."

He added, "The endgame of Chinese communist rule has now begun, I believe, and it has progressed further than many think ... But until the system begins to unravel in some obvious way, those inside of it will play along—thus contributing to the facade of stability."

For Shambaugh, the endemic corruption, the loss of the elite who flee en masse to other countries, and the unstoppable economic slowdown all point to the end of the regime.

"As always in China, there are very reactionary discourses that conceal competent people who can keep the structures together," Jean-Pierre Cabestan counters. "The country is governed by enlightened despots. The government has brought together experts, most notably in economics, who are carefully modernizing the economy."

Along with the People's Republic there is Cuba, whose Communist regime has survived thanks to American opposition to it. How long will we wait until normalization begins? China is propping up North Korea, in spite of friction with the dictatorship in Pyongyang, because it does not want to see another Communist domino fall. No one is willing to place a bet on the party's life span. It could go into overtime for several more decades—or suddenly stumble and fall. No doubt, if that day dawns, the rats will be the first to emerge from their holes to bring down a ruling party that never did anything for them.

EPILOGUE

The rat tribe inspires respect. How could anyone not admire such great tenacity, that unshakable force of character and adaptability, powered by the will to move toward the light by coming to terms with the system, without expecting anything from the state? Everywhere around the world, the Communist countries have created a passive mentality that awakens only when the system begins to fail economically. The conversion of the People's Republic to unbridled capitalism, while maintaining the authoritarian political system guided by a privileged ruling class, has turned these bottom dogs into the kings and queens of getting by.

Living in cities and towns in great numbers, rats prefer damp areas. They can swim up sewers into toilets and take up residence around pipes, behind walls, and near garbage cans. They dig tunnels under the basements of buildings, and make their nests with anything they can repurpose. Most often, they are nocturnal. Besides vegetable and animal matter, they will gnaw on anything they can find: paper, wood, pipes, electric cables. Even some metals, such as copper, lead, and tin, are no match for their teeth.

This sociable omnivore fears solitude and thrives in groups of at least 20, and as large as 200. In a European city like Paris, there are two rats for every person. In the large Asian cities, there are ten for each human. Sewer rats play an important role in processing human waste—without them, sewers and conduits would be plugged up once and for all. In Paris, they devour 800 tons of waste per day. But rat unity and group belonging are based on smell, and their odor and filth feature in many negative expressions: I smell a rat, a dirty rat, ratting someone out, a drowned rat ... And they pay for their intelligence by being laboratory animals, where they learn to modify their behavior to escape traps or find food.

Their bad reputation comes from the damage they inflict— the food stores they devour, or the electric wires they strip. A rat, involuntarily serving as an electrical conductor, may well have been at the source of the short-circuit that caused the cooling systems to shut down at the disabled Fukushima nuclear power plant in Japan in 2013. And think of the diseases they spread: the plague, Lassa fever, leptospirosis, hantavirus ...

However, the nickname "rats" is not entirely pejorative in Chinese culture. Although one of the definitions in *Merriam-Webster's Dictionary* describes a rat as "a contemptible person, such as one who betrays or deserts associates," the Chinese zodiac attributes all sorts of good qualities to it. Chinese astrology describes rats as ambitious, determined, impassioned, intelligent, lively, persuasive, energetic, resourceful, loyal, with a good sense of humor, and generous with friends and family.

"The rat is the first animal in the Chinese zodiac," explains Zhao Shu of the Beijing Research Institute of Culture and History. "In antiquity, to fight against the damage caused by natural catastrophes, humankind's only solution was to have more babies. The rat is known for its exceptional fertility. And rats are everywhere humans are. Their relations are very close. The rat's greatest qualities are its fertility and excellent ability to adapt. It can live in difficult conditions, under water or on land. In Chinese culture, its greatest drawback is that it consumes grain until it can't stand up. Part of its strength is its destructive ability."

"The rat is the smallest animal in the Chinese zodiac," points out Di Yongjun, a historian and researcher at the Chinese Academy of Social Sciences. "He often engages in immoral conduct, but he is very present in Chinese legends. For the Manchus of antiquity, the rat was the greatest, most powerful, and most intelligent of animals. God appreciated him very much and put him first in the zodiac. At the beginning, he and the other eleven animals worked together to protect the country. But as time went by, the rat swelled with pride and stopped concentrating on his work. The other animals complained to the gods, and he was punished for his conduct. He was reduced in size and the cat was sent to keep an eye on him. For the Cantonese and the Tibetans, the rat brings luck when it comes to money. Associated with other Chinese characters, he can also carry a negative image that means frightened, disgusting, or smutty."

"There is no absolute good or bad in Chinese culture," Zhao Shu adds. "If we talk about the rat tribe, it can mean something negative or positive, depending on the context."

But for Di Yongjun, there can be no doubt: "The nickname is a humiliation for people in Beijing who work so hard. They make an important contribution to the city and hope to improve their lot through their efforts."

◆

The Beijing late-summer sky is often torn open by storms and torrential rains, adding to the atmosphere of growing uncertainty. At my Julong Garden residence, many apartments remain empty. Pollution and the weakened economy weigh upon the real estate market.

Armed with their instincts, my rats, the rat people living beneath the building, can feel that nothing good is coming their way. Liu Shuzen, the wife of my friend Zheng Yuanchao, who looks after our complex's maintenance, has lost her eternal smile. I hadn't seen them for several days after a time away for vacation, and I was beginning to worry. What if they had been expelled from Julong while I was in Europe? They would have had to leave without saying goodbye. Her expression clouded by care, her face drawn and sad, Liu feels that the end is near—her mother is hanging on to life by a thread, though her mind has already departed. And Liu knows her own days are numbered at Julong.

"With everything that's happening, the bosses aren't giving us any breaks," she says, her voice flat.

They had both warned me their contract would not be renewed the day management would be forced to pay for their health insurance. They have only a few weeks before that fateful day. Zheng laughs as usual, but his eyes have darkened. It's the first time I have seen them so burdened, despite Zheng's knowing wink, as generous as always, trying to convince me all is well.

Standing at the living room window, I have been watching the rain pour down for hours now, my thoughts elsewhere. I picture the underground residents of Xibahe Zhongli fighting the flood, piling up sandbags to keep their basements from filling up with water. On stormy days in Beijing, I can't keep that picture out of my head.

◆

After a few days, calm returns. The Beijing sky is brilliant blue, something that occurs only once a year. Up on the surface, purified, the streets of the city have been scrubbed clean of the grime made of pollution particles and endless streams of spit. The sun sends down pleasant warmth and golden light upon the office towers. Below, in the city's bowels, the season of mud-streaked hallways has begun.

Notes from a traditional musical instrument come through the open bedroom window. It takes me several hours before I realize that someone is playing the *erhu* in the street. Then I think it might be Xiaoyun, the blind musician from Sanlitun, playing his banged-up, two-stringed "barbarian violin." I go out and head in the direction of the music. A raging jackhammer makes the job difficult. After circling the block, I come upon the musician. It really is Xiaoyun. The Chinese dream he told me about has been broken. He came back early from his tour of provincial villages. One of his two musicians from the band was hit by a car and died. With only two of them remaining, it's impossible for him to get rich playing weddings and funerals.

"People are willing to spend money, but they want a real traditional group. For that, you have to be three," he says, lifting his instrument with a resigned look.

Then he lets fly with a string of swear words because he lost his spot in upscale Sanlitun. Winter in the countryside is too rough for him. He's better off back in Beijing, with its miserable but warm underground.

But he hasn't given up. Xiaoyun is sure—by next spring he will have found another musician to fill out his trio. And he'll get back on the road again, to seek his fortune.

ACKNOWLEDGMENTS

For Jin Duoyou, my accomplice, without whom nothing would have been possible.

For Laetitia, Joséphine, and Antoine, who share this Chinese adventure.

PATRICK SAINT-PAUL has been a correspondent in China for the French newspaper *Le Figaro* since 2013. Over his career he has also covered assignments in Sierra Leone (which won him the Jean Marin Prize for War Correspondents in 2000), Liberia, Sudan, Côte d'Ivoire, Iraq, Afghanistan, and Germany, as well as the Israeli–Palestinian conflict. *The Rat People* is his first book.

DAVID HOMEL is a writer, journalist, filmmaker, translator, and the author of seven novels. He has translated many French-language books into English and is a two-time recipient of the Governor General's Literary Award for Translation. He lives in Montreal.